Easy on the Helm

EASY ON THE HELM

Boat Handling Under Power and Sail

Tom Cunliffe

Illustrated by Tony Garrett

faber and faber

LONDON · BOSTON

First published in 1990
by Faber and Faber Limited
3 Queen Square London WC1N 3AU

Phototypeset by Input Typesetting Ltd, London
Printed in Great Britain by
Richard Clay Ltd, Bungay, Suffolk

A CIP record for this book is available from the British Library

ISBN 0-571-14219-2

Contents

Contents

Contents

List of Illustrations

Introduction

As the title suggests, this book is all about boat handling; at high and low speeds, under power or sail, in tight corners or in open water, in fair weather and foul. It is not a primer, and no attempt is made to explain the basic points of sailing. It has been written for yachtsmen who have been on the water long enough to know what is happening most of the time, and who have learned sufficient to realize where their own shortcomings may lie.

Understanding how a yacht handles under sail is considered by some to be an advanced form of boat handling, but this is a misconception brought upon us by our machine-orientated society. In fact, the only thing a propeller can do that canvas cannot guarantee on every occasion is 'apply the brakes'. Even under power, however, a boat will often pull up unreliably if she is given the chance, behaving like a road vehicle with an oil spillage over the starboard forward brake pads.

The secrets of successful handling vary for different boats in different conditions, but once the general principles have been understood and put into thoughtful operation, a skipper can have confidence in all circumstances. Boat handlers are not born, they are made. More specifically, they make themselves. The competent seaman depends upon broad experience founded on knowledge. The former part of the package is not for sale, though it can be partially substituted by structured exercises, but the latter is there for the taking. This book is designed to make it readily available so that you can fully evaluate the experience you have already acquired, and make every future manoeuvre count positively towards the rapid achievement of real expertise.

Tom Cunliffe

CHAPTER ONE

The Dynamic Balancing Act: Keels, Rudders and Sail Balance

The sole arbiter of direction for a motor vehicle is the steering-wheel. Where the front wheels are pointing, there it will go, unless it is a rally car operating in thick snow.

The skipper of a boat under either power or sail is faced with more subtle possibilities. If the tiller is pushed to starboard the yacht's head will swing to port, so long as all the other forces acting upon her can agree that it should be allowed to. Frequently, however, particularly when under sail at very low speeds or when starting from a standstill, a boat shows no interest in going where she is asked by a skipper whose only instrument of command is the tiller. Almost any boat will turn into the wind if the helm is released when she is sailing at a rate of knots. How rapidly it happens depends on how she is being sailed. When a boat under power is stopped in a strong cross-wind her head will normally 'blow off'. If the operator wants her to turn her bow to windward it may well not be enough to push the helm down and order 'slow ahead'. The only solution, if she refuses to answer, will be to give her more power than would otherwise seem necessary.

These effects and many others are inherent in every boat afloat. Boats differ from one another in the details of their behaviour, but the principles of turning and balance are the same for all of them.

KEELS

Centre of lateral resistance   One of the most important concepts to grasp is that when the rudder is turned in order to alter her heading, a boat swivels around some central pivot point. The stern swings one way, the bows swing the other, and somewhere amidships is a particular spot which, if the boat were not travelling ahead or astern, would not move at all.

I

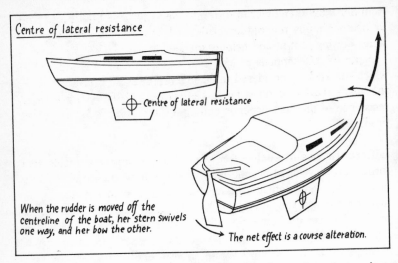

Centre of lateral resistance

Centre of lateral resistance

When the rudder is moved off the centreline of the boat, her stern swivels one way, and her bow the other.

The net effect is a course alteration.

This swivelling effect is more noticeable when a boat is moving slowly. As her speed picks up it will be increasingly difficult to discern, but it is there none the less.

The point around which the boat pivots is called the *centre of lateral resistance*. As its name suggests, it is situated at the focus of the vessel's immersed lateral plane, and it is invariably found somewhere in the keel, more or less amidships. Its exact whereabouts is unimportant in this context, however. What you need to know is that when you shove the tiller over, the stern is going to cartwheel around in that direction (or in the opposite direction to the way you are turning a steering-wheel).

Because the centre of lateral resistance is the nominal point at which resistance to leeway-producing forces is concentrated, any sideways thrust exerted on the forward part of a yacht will encourage her to turn away from it, while any effort exerted aft will induce her to head up. This is of considerable importance when you are balancing a rig for speed and comfort, and it is a vital element of all low-speed manoeuvres, especially under sail.

Keel stall When a boat is under way her keel is always moving through the water at a slight angle because she is making leeway; the effect of this is that the keel develops lift. This lift is assisted by the fact that the boat will be carrying just a touch of *weather helm*, resulting from her inbuilt tendency to turn into the wind. The tiller being held to weather holds the rudder blade to leeward, thus deflecting the water flowing past it, and helping the keel to work.

None of this happens at less than a certain critical speed, below which the keel is considered to be *stalled*. Once the keel has stalled, the boat's rudder becomes far less effective, and the residual lateral resistance of the boat depends entirely on the area of her immersed profile.

Different types of keel   Over the last fifty years the available keel forms have developed beyond recognition. When you are choosing a boat there is now something available to suit your needs ideally, no matter what use you intend for her. Different keel profiles have a profound effect on how efficiently a boat sails, how she handles at high and low speeds, whether or not she is able to look after herself in heavy weather, and how easy her motion will be. The type of keel should be one of the primary considerations for any prospective boat-owner. For any skipper, a knowledge of the various possibilities is the foundation on which he can anticipate the probable behaviour of an unfamiliar yacht.

Straight-line Suzie is a boat of traditional form. Such a vessel will track wonderfully straight, and should be easy to steer at sea, but the long keel which gives her such desirable characteristics is unfortunately not so dynamically efficient as some of the more modern forms. When she is sailing close-hauled she will almost certainly make more leeway than *Winifred the Whizzer*, for example. To offset this, her large lateral area gives her high lateral resistance when her keel is stalled. This means that her options at sea in heavy weather (see Chapter 16) are more numerous than those of some other boats. It also makes her less prone to being blown off-line when approaching a dock in a strong cross-wind. Her heavy displacement will help her in this as well, by supplying her with inertia to resist a gusty wind.

Straight-line Suzie will have a larger turning circle than some of the other boats because the amount of area in the water forward and abaft the pivot point will resist her ability to swivel around. She is also likely to be difficult to steer when going astern.

Capable Clarrie represents a good working compromise. She has

3

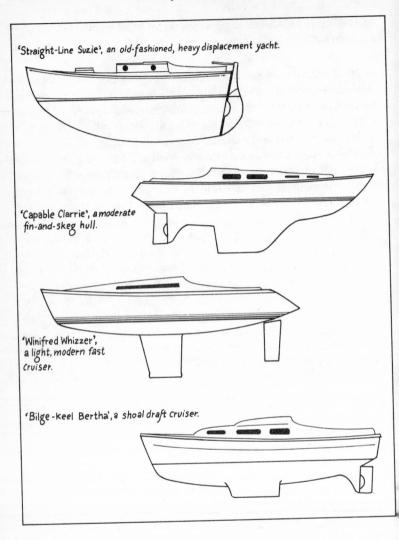

'Straight-Line Suzie', an old-fashioned, heavy displacement yacht.

'Capable Clarrie', a moderate
fin-and-skeg hull.

'Winifred Whizzer',
a light, modern fast
cruiser.

'Bilge-keel Bertha', a shoal draft cruiser.

enough area to grip the water tolerably at low speeds, but her keel is sufficiently refined to deliver a dynamic resistance to leeway that is more than adequate for a cruising yacht. Her cut-away forefoot and the long lever arm between rudder and pivot point promise sharp handling in harbour, but her ability to travel straight at sea may well be inferior to *Straight-line Suzie*'s. When making stern-way she will be less likely to become unmanageable by tripping over the heel of her own keel than will *Suzie*.

Winifred Whizzer, if she has a decent rig, promises to be the most close-winded of all these boats. Her deep, narrow keel delivers tremendous dynamic efficiency, as does her high aspect ratio spade rudder. But with boats, as in life generally, there is no such thing as a free lunch. *Winifred*'s lateral resistance diminishes to next-to-nothing as she slows to sub-stalling speeds. This, coupled with the low inertia of lighter displacement, makes docking in strong winds highly entertaining and can lead to a serious reduction in survival possibilities when she is caught short-handed by storm conditions offshore.

Winifred's large rudder serves her well when it comes to steering a straight course, but it needs to because without it she has little inherent tracking stability, so that steering her in a seaway may be hard work.

Her almost complete lack of immersed lateral area other than her keel means that her ability to swivel about her pivot point is phenom-enal. At moderate speeds she should turn in little more than her own length, and she will be a joy for a muscular individual to steer astern, all of which makes her an easy vessel to manoeuvre at close quarters, unless of course, it is blowing hard.

Bilge-keel Bertha. It is difficult to generalize about bilge-keel yachts because they vary greatly in such vital departments as depth of hull and displacement. *Bertha* is fairly deep-drafted, and so will have a reasonable grip on the water even after her keels have stalled. She will not perform notably to windward, owing to her lack of dynamic efficiency, but she should be steady on the helm. Compared with *Winifred Whizzer* her pivot point is ill-defined and she has considerable immersed lateral area over most of her length. This will make her rather slow to turn in harbours.

FORE-AND-AFT TRIM; MAST RAKE; HELM BALANCE

Fore-and-aft trim   A yacht is intended to float 'to her marks'. If she has been well-designed, the relationship of her sails to her centre

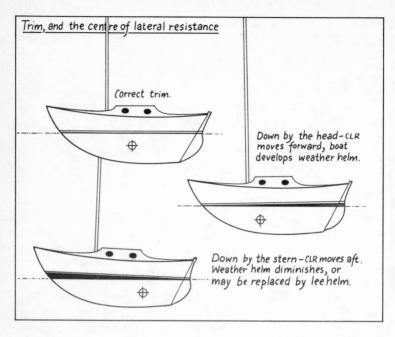

Trim, and the centre of lateral resistance

Correct trim.

Down by the head – CLR moves forward, boat develops weather helm.

Down by the stern – CLR moves aft. Weather helm diminishes, or may be replaced by lee helm.

of lateral resistance will be correct when she is properly trimmed. The result will be a well-mannered vessel.

If the boat is trimmed 'down by the head', however, the centre of lateral resistance will move forward. The stern of the boat will then blow off the wind more easily and more weather helm will be needed to keep her sailing in a straight line. A 'hard-mouthed' boat is the outcome, and the best way of putting things right is to shift some weight aft.

The converse is also true, but not many people complain that their boats have too little weather helm, and so this generally goes unnoticed. If a long down-wind leg is anticipated in a yacht which shows a tendency to develop weather helm, the crew's work-load can be noticeably eased by trimming her down by the stern for the duration of that part of the voyage.

A yacht with a hinged centreboard has an adjustable centre of lateral resistance. With the board right down she realizes her full potential of lateral resistance, which is what she wants as she sails to windward. On a reach, she can bring the board up part of the way,

6

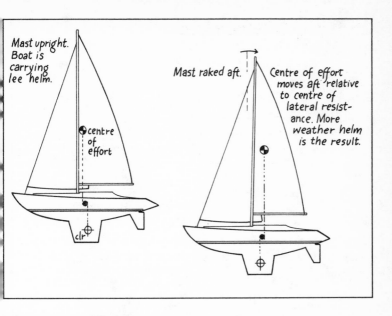

Mast upright. Boat is carrying lee helm.

centre of effort

clr

Mast raked aft. Centre of effort moves aft relative to centre of lateral resistance. More weather helm is the result.

which also has the effect of moving it aft. This shifts her lateral resistance accordingly and helps balance the helm.

Mast rake   Just as a boat's underbody has a centre of lateral resistance, so her sails have a centre of effort. The location of this will vary with sail combination and sheeting angles, but if the designer has been successful the centre of effort will combine with the various other forces acting on the moving boat to produce just a touch of weather helm.

Helm balance   If you are not satisfied with the position of the centre of effort on, say, a sloop, it can often be adjusted by altering the rake of the mast. Yachts with a higher performance rating are equipped with an adjustable backstay so as to encourage crews to do this as a matter of course for different points of sailing. A little weather helm helps a boat to windward, so the mast can be raked aft when the breeze is before the beam (hardening the backstay will also help to keep the jib luff tight); downwind, the less helm the better, so the spar is encouraged to stand upright once more.

HEELING AND ROLLING EFFECTS
ON STEERING

When a sailing boat rolls, or heels, she experiences two entirely different forces, both of which affect her steering characteristics.

Heeling As she heels away from the wind, the driving force of her rig moves outboard and away from the mid-line of the boat. Once the sails are off-centre from the line of the boat's progress they try to screw her around into the wind. The helmsman counters this tendency by applying weather helm (pulling the tiller to windward). As the boat heels further, this propensity for rounding up will increase at a steady rate, but in the case of a boat of moderate design it is unlikely to cause too much in the way of hard work, until the boat is so far over that the helmsman's mind becomes concentrated on other matters. However, in the 1980s, a design trend has appeared which aggravates this effect.

Many modern sailing boats have achieved a large accommodation space by increasing their beam to a higher proportion of their waterline

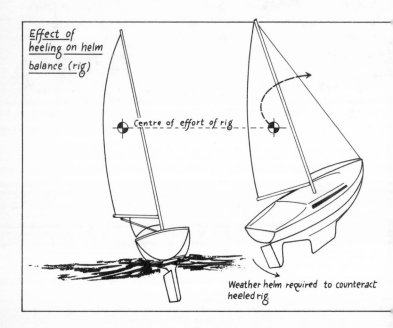

Effect of heeling on helm balance (rig)

Centre of effort of rig

Weather helm required to counteract heeled rig.

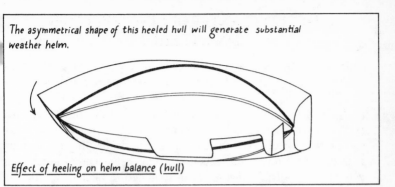

The asymmetrical shape of this heeled hull will generate substantial weather helm.

<u>Effect of heeling on helm balance (hull)</u>

length than has formerly been the norm. In this context, the effect of such beam on the comparatively flat-floored yachts in which it is often found is that the immersed form of the heeled hull becomes so asymmetrical that much helm-heaving is required to keep the show on the road.

More traditional vessels do not suffer from this difficulty. Indeed, some pre-war designers, notably Dr Harrison Butler, specialized in yachts whose sections were of such sophistication that, within reasonable limits, the degree of heel had absolutely no effect on their helm balance. Such yachts were a dream to steer at sea, but were of course cramped for the party-goer.

Rolling When a yacht is rolling heavily, the effect of her rig and changing immersed hull form will generate alternating weather and lee helm. The driver of a beamy, flat-floored boat will need to keep his wits about him as he swings downwind in hard weather, because if he allows the yacht to roll too far he may lose control quite suddenly. All could then be lost as she broaches comprehensively.

STEERING WITH THE SAILS

Even when a boat is stalled or starting from a standstill, she can still be steered. She still has a pivot point, although it may have become rather spongy, and, if she has more than one sail, she has the capacity to apply force both forward and abaft it.

When a boat is lying beam-on to the wind, her natural tendency is

9

Steering with sails

Sheet in main, spill jib, and boat tends to luff up.

Harden in jib sheet, spill wind from main, and boat tends to bear away.

wind

for her head to fall away. This can be counteracted by 'bringing on' the mainsheet. As the sail begins to draw, the yacht's head will be forced up to weather. If it looks as though she will come up too far before the rudder has established a grip on the water, the situation can be controlled by hauling in the jib sheet so that the sail holds the yacht's head down while she gathers way.

A boat can be encouraged to luff by assisting her to heel by hauling in the mainsheet, while the cause of bearing away rapidly is doubly served by letting it out. Not only will this get rid of all power abaft the pivot point, it will also tend to bring the yacht more upright and lessen the tendency to luff due to heeling.

When she is moving well through the water with her keel and rudder firing on all cylinders, a modern boat will often sail controllably under mainsail or jib alone. Some will even develop weather helm with nothing but a genoa. This apparent contradiction in terms is explained by the heeling of the boat, but the general point to remember is this: any sail setting abaft the pivot point is encouraging the boat to turn to windward, while any sail forward is trying to persuade her to bear away.

The ramifications of this simple statement pervade all boat handling under sail, whether you are crossing the Pacific on a fast broad reach, hove to in a Biscay gale, or manoeuvring through a crowded anchorage to a suitable berth. Acting upon it can save time and wear-and-tear when on passage. In harbour, it will make the difference between tidy manoeuvres and hit-and-miss, sling-her-in-and-hope-for-the-best attempts. Mostly such ill-informed efforts end up in the 'miss' category, and the 'hits' show a nasty tendency to turn out expensively.

CHAPTER TWO

Theory of Sail-Power

Back in the 1950s, sailing a sloop was a simple business. All you had to do was choose your sails, pull them up hard, sheet them until their luffs stopped lifting, and glide away into the sunset. A few minor rig adjustments were becoming available, such as moveable jib sheet fairleads and adjustable mainsail clew outhauls, but essentially there was little that could be done to alter the shape of the sails. They were cut to a form somewhere between what the owner thought he wanted and what the sail-maker was sure he ought to have. That became their shape, and there it stayed until old age or honest abuse blew them out of it, and drove the owner back to the loft for another ten rounds with the palm-and-needle boys.

Time has changed all that. Even on cruising boats we now have sails whose shape can be adjusted within certain broad limits to suit any conditions in which they are capable of being set. The majority of today's yachts are equipped with the necessary gear to effect these changes, and the net result is that our rigs can develop far more usable power than their predecessors.

But there is a catch.

The catch is that if we fail to use this gear to its best advantage, it can actually work against us. A stretch-luff genoa improperly set up in a stiff breeze will be far less effective than its old-fashioned 'grind-it-up-tight-and-go-for-broke' equivalent. However, in able hands, the modern sail will lift the boat higher to windward and make her heel far less. It depends on the user. Similarly, we've all seen those amazing pictures of yachts racing before the days of the centre boom-vang. The twist on the mainsails looks unbelievable to our eyes, with what appears to be half the wind being ditched without ceremony from the upper portion of the sails. Now we have controls for checking the boom's tendency to rise; but how much should we be controlling it?

Heave too hard on the vang at the wrong time and the boat is killed just as efficiently as it was by the absence of a vang altogether. We need to get it right.

This sort of talk isn't to do with tuning hot-shot racers; it is about giving a cruiser a decent, seamanlike chance to perform properly and award her people a smooth, quiet ride. A yacht with properly trimmed sails not only goes faster (and may thus save her tide, anchor before sunset, tie up before the pubs shut, or whatever else motivates you to move it along), she also travels more comfortably.

Until the operation of a modern rig is fully understood, it cannot be used effectively to slow the boat down. Unlike the driver of a motor-car, a sailor needs to be able to go fast before he can fully control the boat moving slowly. So here goes! We'll start with how a sail actually works, and progress from there.

SAILS

It is obvious to anyone who has ever looked at a sail when it is set that it is not a flat piece of canvas. It is cunningly cut and stitched so that it has curvature as well as length and breadth. What is not so clear is how this triangle of cloth propels a boat in any direction other than dead down-wind. The basic misconception normally held by the laity is that a sail is a bag to catch the breeze. 'The wind puffs into the bag,' they fondly imagine, 'and the yacht is blown along.'

In reality, unless the boat is on a dead run, this is not so. When the sail is set properly the wind blows smoothly around both sides of the curved cloth. As it does so the sail generates lift by forming a zone of low pressure on its leeward, or convex side, into which the boat is effectively sucked.

It is easier to understand how this is achieved if, instead of thinking of the air flowing past the sail as the colourless gas that it is, we imagine it as two lines of table-tennis balls flying along in pairs. As they arrive at the luff of the sail the two lines are separated so that one ball of each pair flies around the convex side, and the other the concave side. Shortly after they have cleared the leech of the sail, each ball joins up with its opposite number once again and disappears from the picture, having done its job well. All that appears to have happened is that the streams of balls have been parted from one another, and deflected in direction. A further analogy will clarify how this contrives to generate a pressure difference.

Instead of table-tennis balls flying around the sail, imagine two ranks of soldiers marching down a straight road, one rank on either side of the road, and each soldier abeam of his opposite number. The files approach a bend in the road. As they negotiate the turn, the soldiers on the outside lengthen their stride and accelerate in order to maintain station opposite their buddies, while the soldiers on the inside shorten theirs and slow down.

Now go back to the table-tennis balls. As they fly around the curved sail, the ones on the leeward, or outside, of the sail accelerate just as the soldiers did, and the ones on the inside slow down or, if they are cutting the corner, maintain pace. As the outside balls speed up they spread out one from another. There are fewer of them to the square metre of sail now, so they exert less pressure than their colleagues on the other side. Substitute the idea of the little white balls by the concept of molecules of air dashing about, and you have the answer: a pressure difference is established across the sail.

THE SLOT EFFECT

Where two sails are used in conjunction with each other, the power of the system is increased by something greater than the extra area which is on offer. The air that is passing in front of a genoa is the same as that which is about to be accelerated round the back of the mainsail. This airstream is also being squeezed through the gap, or slot, between the two sails. Any flowing gas that is compressed in this way is accelerated by the *venturi effect*, so the air that is coming around the back of the genoa, creating the lift on that sail, will also have to speed up, pro rata, in order to keep pace with events. The whole rushing mass then rips around the lee side of the mainsail, whose effect is pepped up dramatically.

In practice, seamen have known about this for generations, but just to make sure it was not a myth a series of experiments was performed some years ago by a reputable scientific organization. A strain gauge was connected to a genoa sheet in a wind tunnel, and the force on the sheet was noted. When a mainsail was set up in the correct place abaft the genoa, the strain on the headsail sheet was observed to rise considerably. Q E D.

SAIL-POWER AND FORWARD PROGRESS

The lifting force generated by a sail is in a direction approximately at right angles to a line joining luff and leech. On the face of things this suggests that a close-hauled yacht should be blown almost sideways. The reason why this does not happen is that she has no desire to go that way on account of her keel and her general resistance to sideways forces. She is anxious to oblige by going ahead, if at all possible.

The force of the close-hauled sail can be resolved into two smaller forces: a forward component and a sideways component. These two forces acting simultaneously would produce an identical effect to the actual force of the sail. The diagram shows that when the yacht's sails are sheeted close to her mid-line the forward component is far less than its sideways partner. However, such is the lateral resistance of a well-designed sailing vessel that she is able to soak up nearly all the sideways force, leaving the diminutive forward component to work its magic against the yacht's equally small resistance to forward movement. And away you go!

Unfortunately, the whole of the sideways component of the force of the rig can never be gobbled up by the yacht's keel. Broadly speaking, the residue is manifested as leeway and the heeling of the vessel. The more efficient the keel and the rig, the less are the heeling and leeway, and the more effective the forward push.

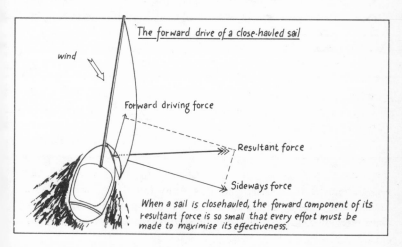

The forward drive of a close-hauled sail

wind

Forward driving force

Resultant force

Sideways force

When a sail is closehauled, the forward component of its resultant force is so small that every effort must be made to maximise its effectiveness.

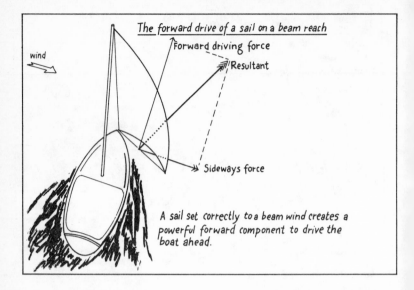

The forward drive of a sail on a beam reach

wind

Forward driving force

Resultant

Sideways force

A sail set correctly to a beam wind creates a powerful forward component to drive the boat ahead.

As the wind moves aft and sails are sheeted further from the centre-line of the boat, the forward component of the sails increases while the sideways force diminishes. Once the apparent wind (see Chapter 7) is established just abaft the beam, the sails can drive with maximum efficiency until the wind comes so far aft that they can no longer be sheeted to allow the air to flow around them properly. At this point, they become no more than the wind-bags of the layman's fancy, and the boat slows down on to a dead run.

This is all very well, but it only works as long as the air is flowing cleanly around the sail. Once the airstream detaches itself on one side or the other, the 'pairs of soldiers' will no longer remain opposite each other, the 'table-tennis balls' will not rejoin their opposite numbers at the leech of the sail, and the whole lift-generating mechanism will break down.

There are three main states of sail trim:

Under-sheeted In this condition either the sheet has been eased too far or, if the boat is close-hauled, she is being steered too close to the wind. The effect is that the luff of the sail 'lifts' and the airflow breaks down, particularly on the windward side.

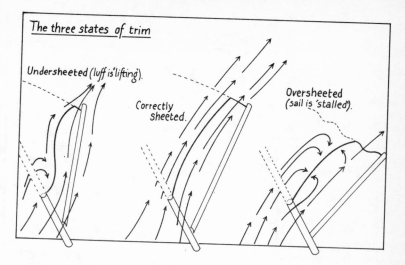

The three states of trim

Undersheeted (luff is 'lifting').

Correctly sheeted.

Oversheeted (sail is 'stalled').

Correctly sheeted Here, everything is working fine, and the sail is pulling as well as it is able.

Over-sheeted When the sail is sheeted too close to the boat's centre-line, or when a close-hauled boat is steered below (to leeward of) her best course to windward, the sail is said to *stall*. It may look correctly set, but air is breaking away from its leeward side. In this condition the sail is producing minimal lift and an overdose of the dreaded leeway and heeling.

Constant vigilance is required aboard any yacht to ensure that her sails are correctly sheeted. On a racing boat the matter is receiving continuous attention. Depending upon circumstances and the character of the individual, the cruising skipper will certainly compromise from this ideal, but no sailor worthy of the name will sail for hours with the genoa apparently full without easing the sheet periodically to check for stalling. After a while this becomes second nature, and a matter of personal pride. The very thought of great chunks of air whirling around all over the place only a few feet off the deck, when the whole should be in harmonious flow, ought to spoil any seaman's day.

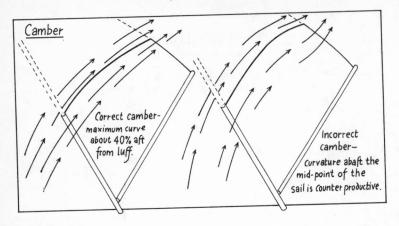

Camber

Correct camber—
maximum curve
about 40% aft
from luff.

Incorrect
camber—
Curvature abaft the
mid-point of the
sail is counter productive.

SAIL CAMBER

We have discussed how the lift of a sail derives from the fact that it offers a curved surface to the airstream. The deeper the curvature, the more the air-flow will be bent and, so long as the air does not detach from the sail, the greater will be the power of the system.

The most notable difference between the sails of today and their antecedents is that we now have the ability to control the state of their curvature, or *camber*. In light airs a deep camber may be required, while in stronger winds it will be desirable to flatten the same sail so that it will not over-power the boat. All this is possible with modern gear.

The point of maximum camber must be maintained in the correct fore-and-aft position. For a genoa, this is generally about 40 per cent – 45 per cent of the distance from luff to leech. A mainsail set abaft a headsail may prefer its camber at 50 per cent, but no sail, in any circumstances, should be carried when its camber moves irreversibly further aft than that. At this point, the sail will be so inefficient as to be a gross embarrassment to the yacht's performance.

The way camber is adjusted in practice will be studied in Chapter 3, but first we will take a look at how a boat keeps herself pointing in the right direction, because if she is not sailing steadily on her course, any attempt to set up the rig is going to be a waste of time.

CHAPTER THREE

Letting Her Go

'Oh Lord, let her go!' was the anguished cry aboard many a nine-teenth-century sailing ship as the shellbacks groaned to see their charge being poorly sailed by the skipper. Paradoxically, the same phrase was uttered in joy from time to time as the Old Man got it right in a strong breeze and a thousand tons of clipper thundered away at 15 knots, but it must be said that even in those halcyon days sails were often set less well than they might have been. No doubt as a ship slugged along at 7 knots when 10 should have been the mark the sea-lawyers would smirk and say, 'More days, more dollars', but that would do little to cheer the spirits of the real sailors. A vessel doing less well than she could have done was anathema to them, just as she ought to be to us.

This does not necessarily mean that we should be risking the safety of our yachts by desperate driving. What we want is to see our boats sailed in such a way that they can deliver us to our destination in as short a time and in as great a degree of comfort as they are reasonably able.

We have dealt with the essential theory in the previous two chapters. In this one we will examine how to deal with the sails so that a yacht can do herself justice.

CONTROL OF CAMBER

Before a sail can be *trimmed* effectively it must be the right *shape* for the day on which it is set. In the case of a headsail this is achieved by adjusting its *camber* and its *twist*. The only effective control of **headsail camber** on a cruising yacht is halyard tension. As the halyard winch is wound on harder the camber of the sail moves forward; as it is eased off, the camber moves aft. How dramatic this movement is depends on the sail, but all soft-luffed sails are affected to a certain extent.

Camber is best checked by looking up at the mid-part of the sail. If it has a 'go faster stripe' the job is easy. If there is no stripe the curvature of the sail can be judged well enough by reference to the seams.

The sail should be hoisted, then sheeted in a close-hauled state before deciding how much tension to apply. If the breeze is light the halyard should be wound up *gently*, watching the sail all the time. When the camber is about 45 per cent aft from the luff, that will do.

As the wind strength increases, the camber will be 'blown' aft as the sail stretches. Once this begins to happen, the halyard should be cranked up harder until sail shape is restored. At even higher wind speeds, the tension is further increased; at this stage it may be found necessary to move the sheet fairlead aft (see following section) so that the camber remains where it should be as the sail is flattened right off.

When the wind has risen to a degree where no amount of tweaking can maintain the sail in the shape it should be, it is time to change down to a smaller, flatter-cut sail, or take a few rolls if it is roller-reefed. If the sail has been expertly made and the sail wardrobe is well-planned, this moment will coincide with the point at which the boat can no longer carry that area of sail, no matter how well cut it may be.

Mainsail camber   is controlled by luff tension in just the same way as that of a headsail, but because it is set on a boom, a mainsail usually enjoys the additional facility of a clew outhaul. The two are used in conjunction to achieve the desired result, remembering that the camber of the main is often best when it is only fractionally forward of the middle of the sail. One of the reasons for this is that if the camber is too far forward, the sail will have what is called a 'hard entry', which may cause it to be back-winded by the air coming through the slot. This is more noticeable when a boat is masthead rigged. The fractional-rig mainsail is often cut to carry its camber further forward, to the 40 per cent mark.

The way to find the best result is to experiment and *look*. The camber must never be abaft the centre of the sail and, ideally, no part of the sail should be back-winded when the boat is close-hauled. This

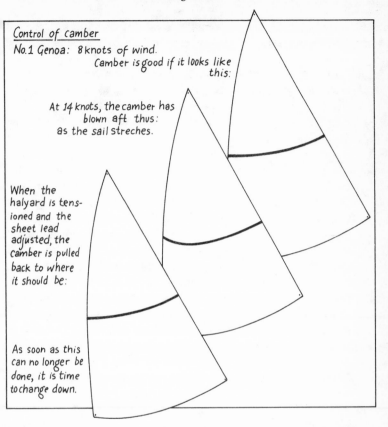

Control of camber

No.1 Genoa: 8 knots of wind.
Camber is good if it looks like this:

At 14 knots, the camber has blown aft thus: as the sail streches.

When the halyard is tensioned and the sheet lead adjusted, the camber is pulled back to where it should be:

As soon as this can no longer be done, it is time to change down.

latter proposition may sometimes be compromised, but NEVER the former.

Some boats have no easy method of adjusting the clew outhaul, but it is usually possible on smaller boats to heave the clew in and out by hand. If this is not convenient, a healthy compromise will be required on the question of foot tension.

The Cunningham hole is to be found a foot or so above the mainsail tack on some cruiser-racers. A line passed through this can be hauled down in order to increase a luff tension without touching the halyard winch. A 'Cunningham' is important if a boat is racing because it allows the luff of the main to be tensioned when to wind up the halyard any further would mean raising the head of the sail above the measured mark on the mast, with a resulting risk of penalty.

Flattening reefs are often built into high-performance cruising sails. A 'flattener' has only one cringle, found in the leech of the sail. It is used on occasions when the sail is too full for the prevailing conditions, but not yet so oversized that a reef is needed. It works by taking out the fullness from the foot of the sail.

Leech-lines are to be found in the majority of today's cruising sails. Put bluntly, these pieces of string are, for most of us, a necessary evil. The leech-line in either a jib or a mainsail is there to ensure that the leech does not flutter, and is not 'hooked' either. The way it can best achieve this for a given sail shape is to slack away until the leech begins to beat, then bring it on again just sufficiently to put the sail to sleep, and no further. On some sails leech-lines are big on nuisance value, requiring considerable attention, but without them our nights would be sleepless as our leeches beat themselves noisily to expensive destruction.

TWIST

You will have noticed that most boats seem to exhibit a certain amount of *twist* between the angle of attack of the bottom and top of their sails. This is not a matter of chance. It does not occur because it is impossible to control a sail well enough to stop it happening (it used to, but it doesn't any more); it is an important consideration in the search for boat speed and should be watched carefully.

A sail needs to twist because the apparent wind (see Chapter 7) which it is bending is blowing at different speeds 10ft and 30ft above the water. Surface friction between the flowing air and the sea's face is slowing down the breeze at deck-level more than it is at the masthead. The slower the airstream, the more the speed of the boat modifies it in strength and direction. Since the boat's movement is tending to pull the wind angle forward, the lower part of the sail will require to be sheeted closer to her centre-line than the upper part if the whole sail is to set sweetly. The amount of twist required for a given sail will depend on the wind speed, so sails require adjustment to take it into account.

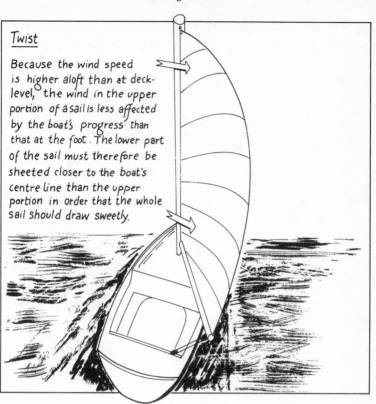

Twist

Because the wind speed is higher aloft than at deck-level, the wind in the upper portion of a sail is less affected by the boat's progress than that at the foot. The lower part of the sail must therefore be sheeted closer to the boat's centre line than the upper portion in order that the whole sail should draw sweetly.

Headsails The twist of a headsail (and to a certain extent the camber, as noted above), is controlled by the fore and aft position of the sheet fairlead. The primary sources of visual information on the subject are luff tell-tales. Every modern boat should have three or four of these lengths of wool evenly spaced up the luffs of her jibs, 5 or 6in abaft the luff-tape, or rope. If your sails do not have them, they can be installed in minutes with a palm and needle. 8-in lengths of one-ply darning wool are punched through the sail, and knotted on either side of the cloth.

All that is required to set the fairlead correctly is to sheet the sail close-hauled, steer on the wind and look at the tell-tales. You'll have started out with the fairlead placed so that the imaginary line drawn onwards from the sheet into the sail meets the luff about 40 per cent

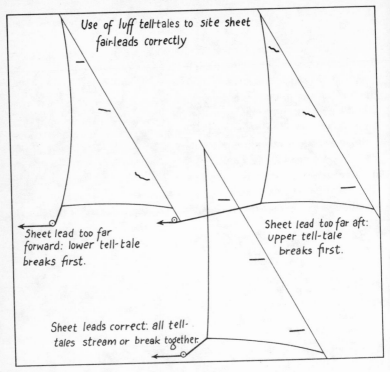

Use of luff tell-tales to site sheet fair-leads correctly

Sheet lead too far forward: lower tell-tale breaks first.

Sheet lead too far aft: upper tell-tale breaks first.

Sheet leads correct: all tell-tales stream or break together.

of the way from tack to head. If all is well, the tell-tales will be streaming cleanly aft on both sides of the sail. Note what happens if the boat is pointed too 'high': the windward, or inside, tell-tales will lift and begin to break well before the luff of the sail crumples. If the boat is stalled by steering too far off the wind, the tell-tales on the lee side will collapse, indicating that air has broken away from outside the sail (Chapter 2). If the twist of the sail is incorrect, one windward tell-tale will break before the others when the boat is brought steadily towards the wind.

When the bottom tell-tale goes first, it shows that the lower portion of the sail is too full. This can be cured by moving the fairlead further aft so as to flatten the foot of the sail and 'open' the leech. On the other hand, if the lead is too far aft, the sheet will be pulling the foot of the sail into a board-like shape, while the upper sections will be twisting off, lacking the necessary leech tension to form them properly. This state is indicated by the upper windward tell-tales lifting before the others, and is cured, needless to say, by sliding the fairlead forward a few notches.

Once the sheets are eased and the boat is reaching, the tell-tales are used to achieve the optimum *set*, but remember that as the boat bears away the apparent wind speed may alter sufficiently to render the luff tension too great. This will spoil the shape of the sail. It only takes a second or two to ease the halyard, and if this wins you ¼ knot of boat speed, remember, that is worth 1 hour in 24 at 6 knots!

Further control over the flow of air across a headsail can be achieved by using a *barber-hauler*. Sometimes, try as you will, you cannot set up the shape you want without, for example, backwinding the mainsail. This can be particularly annoying on a close reach. A way to cure the situation is to rig a line from the clew of the sail, outboard to a block on the toe-rail, thence to a spare winch in the cockpit. The sheet is eased an inch or two and this new line, or barber-hauler, is brought into play to heave the clew of the sail further from the boat's mid-line. The effect is to 'open the slot' without compromising the shape of the genoa. Most cruisers do not enjoy the facilities for such refinements of sail shape, but where they exist, they can be genuinely effective over a long leg of a passage.

Mainsails Luff tell-tales do not work at all well on mainsails because the presence of the mast interferes with the airflow over that portion of the sail. However, it is useful to know how cleanly air is running off the leech. If the leech is hooked to windward, for example, eddies will form around it which will slam on the air-brakes with deadly efficiency. Some sails arrive from the sail-makers with leech tell-tales built in. If yours does not, a few 4-in lengths of light fabric tape sewn into the outboard ends of the batten pockets will serve perfectly. Twist in mainsails is easily controlled, readily spotted, and affects not only boat speed, but also helm balance. Too little twist at the wrong time will pile up weather helm mercilessly as well as slowing you down. A modicum of attention paid to this department of the wind engine will repay your trouble many times over.

Mainsail twist can be judged roughly by a quick check of how the curve of the leech is following that of the headsail. A finer gauge is found by looking up the after part of the sail from beneath the boom. If the top batten is running parallel to the boom itself, you have a good compromise. At that point the leech tell-tales will probably all be flying free. If they are not – and generally it is the upper ones that misbehave – then it is time to attend to the twist of the sail.

The most important all-round controls of mainsail twist are the centre boom-vang and the mainsheet. Both regulate leech tension. The sheet also adjusts the *trim* of the sail (how far it is set from the centre-line of the boat) for much of the time, but when the yacht is close-hauled or close-reaching, this is taken care of by the *traveller*, leaving the sheet free to shape the leech.

When the sail is close-hauled, the sheet is pulling more or less down on the leech. If the boom-vang is let off, the sheet itself will check the amount the boom-end rises, and so control twist.

Once the desired shape has been obtained with sheet, halyard and outhaul, the sail's angle of attack is set by sliding the sheet blocks along the traveller. In light airs with a big genoa set, you may find that in order to stop the mainsail luff lifting while keeping the tell-tales flying, the boom needs to be placed on, or almost on, the centre-line of the boat. This is perfectly acceptable. What will not do is for the boom to move to windward of the centre-line. This demand does not, however, apply to the sheet-block on the traveller. Often, in very

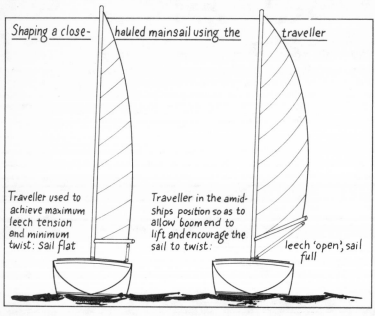

Shaping a close-hauled mainsail using the traveller

Traveller used to achieve maximum leech tension and minimum twist: sail flat

Traveller in the amid-ships position so as to allow boom end to lift and encourage the sail to twist:

leech 'open', sail full

light going, the desired twist can only be found by pulling the block well to windward of amidships and easing the sheet so that the boom rises on to the mid-line.

As the breeze hardens the sail will twist more, just when you probably want it to twist less. When this happens, you heave down on the sheet, usually hardening the halyard to firm up the camber at the same time. The sail will now be considerably flatter and you will probably find that the sheet-block can be dropped down the traveller to leeward. This will have the double benefit of providing more forward drive (see Chapter 2) and also easing the helmsman's pain by reducing the boat's tendency to heel and round up to windward.

In windy weather when a small headsail is set and the main is well reefed, it may even pay to let the sheet block run right down to the bottom of the traveller while going to windward.

On a racing yacht the centre boom-vang may be in use when close-hauled to help flatten the bunt of the mainsail, but on a cruising yacht this is rarely necessary. This control comes into its own when trim considerations on a reach or run have called for the mainsheet to be eased 'beyond the end of the traveller'. Because of its shorter lever

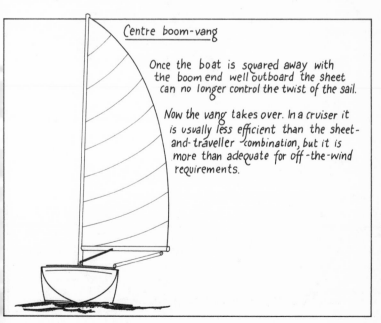

Centre boom-vang

Once the boat is squared away with the boom end well outboard the sheet can no longer control the twist of the sail.

Now the vang takes over. In a cruiser it is usually less efficient than the sheet-and-traveller combination, but it is more than adequate for off-the-wind requirements.

arm, the vang will not control the leech of the sail as successfully as did the sheet, but by this time the forward component of the rig has increased sufficiently for the whole business of sail shape and trim to be somewhat less critical.

Finally, a word of warning: the top leech tell-tale on a high aspect ratio (tall and narrow) mainsail can be a demon to put to sleep. Don't forget that you're out there for fun and the thing will spoil your day if you let it. It is only there as a guide. So long as that batten is in the right sort of alignment you won't go far wrong.

Do not forget, the traveller is there to *trim* the sail when you are close-hauled or close-reaching. On these points of sailing, the task of the mainsheet is to *shape* it.

Set up with these guidelines in the skipper's mind, a boat will always give of her best on passage. She will go fast, she will be easy on her helmsmen, and she will heel far less, all of which combine to encourage the great cruising virtues: comfort, speed, and low-stress yachting.

CHAPTER FOUR

Shortening Sail

In the last chapter we discussed how to help a yacht to move as well as she can under full sail, but there comes a time, however well the rig is set up, when every boat is over-pressed by this amount of canvas. That is the time to shorten down.

SIGNS THAT A BOAT IS OVER-PRESSED

Excessive angle of heel is the most obvious pointer to the fact that it is time to reduce canvas. When the toe-rail disappears under the water most boats are not only becoming extremely uncomfortable, they are also sailing less efficiently. The further the boat heels, the more her keel is struggling to grip the water, and the more leeway she will make.

Sea state has a considerable effect on how far a boat can be allowed to heel. In calm water she can drag her rail through the gusts if she is in a hurry, whereas in a heavy sea she will fall off every wave and bury her decks to the hatches. Not only is this stressful for her victims, it also threatens to shake the rig to pieces.

Potential rig damage is less of a problem with modern equipment than it was in days gone by. The gear on a well-found yacht will stand even if she is blown down on to her beam ends. This was not always so; sailors in pre-war, pre-polyester and pre-stainless steel yachts had always to consider the possibility that if they drove a boat too hard, they might tear the stick clean out of her.

While the wind alone may do little damage to yachts today, the lurch of an over-pressed vessel crashing hard off a steep wave may provide a snatching force that is enough to break something. It does not do to become over-confident of one's gear.

Weather helm increases with heel, and excess weather helm is usually the most unambiguous indication that it is time to reef or change down. On the beamy, flat-floored boats favoured by many designers of production cruisers, weather helm often increases drastically as the boat leans away from the wind. In some cases, it suddenly becomes so extreme that the yacht takes charge and flies up into the wind, despite the best efforts of a good helmsman to control her. Long before this stage is reached, the helm will be telling the experienced skipper that it's time something was done to ease the boat.

The available options are to reduce headsail area by either rolling in a reef or changing down, to reef the mainsail, or to reef or drop the mizzen if there is one. What you decide to do will depend on the boat and the circumstances. If you are carrying a large, full-cut headsail, for instance, it usually pays to exchange it for a flatter, smaller alternative. If your boat is equipped with a well-cut furling genoa, a few rolls in that is by far the easiest first reduction. However, if the headsail is not over-powering the boat, it is usually best to put a reef in the mainsail. This helps in two ways: it reduces sail area and lowers the centre of effort of the rig, thus diminishing the tendency for the boat to heel. Also, by moving the clew inboard along the boom, it shifts the centre of effort of the sail *forward* and closer to the yacht's centre of pivot (Chapter 2). This reduces her desire to luff, and eases the weather helm as it does so.

The process of reducing sail can be all joy and ease, or it can be a horror show from which all hands recoil, and which the skipper puts off until matters have become so desperate that Sinbad himself would turn away if invited to go forward to the halyard winch. The choice is in the skipper's gift.

First, he needs to be completely at home with his gear, and secondly, he must know how to handle his boat so that the job can be done without needless drama.

REEFING THE MAINSAIL

Given that the wind is forward of the beam so that the sail can spill wind, the secret of reefing any mainsail is to have a *routine*. Presented with the correct sequence of actions any sail will lie down like a lamb;

ut woe to the sailor who does things in the wrong order. He ends
up doing battle with an untamed beast.

Slab reefing For good reason this is the most popular system of
reefing. It is quick, kind to the sail, and it results in a fine set once
the reef is in. This is the sequence:

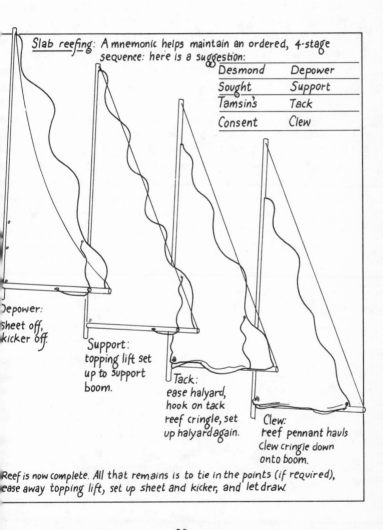

Slab reefing: A mnemonic helps maintain an ordered, 4-stage sequence: here is a suggestion:

Desmond	Depower
Sought	Support
Tamsin's	Tack
Consent	Clew

Depower:
sheet off,
kicker off.

Support:
topping lift set
up to support
boom.

Tack:
ease halyard,
hook on tack
reef cringle, set
up halyard again.

Clew:
reef pennant hauls
clew cringle down
onto boom.

Reef is now complete. All that remains is to tie in the points (if required), ease away topping lift, set up sheet and kicker, and let draw.

* Release the vang and sheet to de-power the sail.
* Top up the boom with the topping-lift. This ensures that the boom doesn't brain the cockpit gang when the halyard is released. It also relieves the weight of the spar from the leech of the sail, which makes hauling down the clew cringle much easier. Many boats with rigid, hydraulically operated boom-vangs do not have a topping-lift; in which case, the same effect is achieved by pumping up the vang until it has the weight.
* Ease away the halyard, and secure the tack cringle on the hook, or lash it to the boom gooseneck.
* Set up the halyard to ensure that the tack stays on the hook.
* Haul down the clew cringle using the correct reefing pennant, which should be permanently rove. In small craft this may be done by a straight pull, but in a vessel of any tonnage a winch or a tackle will be required.
* Ease the topping-lift, set up the kicker and sheet in.
* The reef can now be tied in using points if fitted, or a lacing if they are not. On many modern vessels, tying in the reef is a sophistication that is not required except in unusually hard weather, or on occasions when the yacht is 'on show'. Indeed, the increasingly popular fully battened mainsail self-stows in its lazy-jacks, requiring no attention whatever other than to pull down tack and clew. In the case of an old-fashioned boat with a long boom, however, it will be found necessary to tie in the reef every time.

Roller reefing The method of reefing by rolling the boom round while easing the main halyard is rarely seen nowadays. Historically, it was used on gaff-rigged pilot cutters a century ago and worked very well, given the accepted trade-off in poor sail shape. From those days through into the 1960s it was used on some yachts, but it was never truly satisfactory after the introduction of the Bermudan, or three-cornered, mainsail. On these rigs, the sail tended to become fuller as it was reefed more deeply, which is the opposite of what is desirable. Also, the boom end often drooped ever lower, threatening the skull integrity of the cockpit crew. Specially shaped booms, or the addition of tapered battens to their outboard ends, helped considerably, but once modern slab reefing with winches and tack hooks became available, the death-knell of roller reefing was sounded, amid sighs of general relief.

The technique of roller reefing is logical:
* Unlace the reefing line, if one is fitted (this secures the lower part of the luff to the slides in the mast groove).
* Remove the centre boom-vang from the boom.
* Top up, and roll away.
* As in slab reefing, the sail should ideally be spilling wind as it is reefed.

Other methods The introduction of a variety of systems whereby the mainsail is both stowed and reefed by rolling it totally or partially into the mast has revolutionized sail-handling. Sad to say, apparent nautical cure-alls generally hide a frowning countenance behind their smiling faces. These reefing arrangements are frequently expensive, the masts which house them are bulky, and failure of the mechanics can cause the proud owner considerable grief and woe. No doubt time will ultimately make a good job of in-mast reefing systems; it will also offer electrical or hydraulic sail-handling from the comfort of the skipper's double-bunk, at which point the harassed child of the technological revolution will probably ask himself why he's bothering at all. When the light dawns upon him I believe that, unless he is geriatric, he will rid himself of all such items. They serve, after all, only to insulate him from the reality of his meeting with the elements, and if he craves nothing but ever greater protection from his chosen environment, he would do well to consider the benefits of motor-yachting.

It seems a pity to spend all that money on a sail and then never to handle it.

SMOOTHING THE WAY

The handling of a boat while a reef is being taken will make all the difference for the crew. If you get it right the job will be done quickly, so that the foredeck crowd will shamble aft, still dry, and without having had to hang on like rodeo riders on fireworks day.

The answer is either to slow the boat down or stop her altogether. A minimum of time will be lost because if the hands are properly organized it should not take more than a couple of minutes to reef the mainsail on a 38-ft sloop. A full racing crew worthy of their salt will do the job in twenty seconds.

Think about that.

Just before she is reefed, a 32-footer sailing to windward will be leaping along at 6 knots or so, throwing spray around. Her foredeck will not be an enjoyable place to be, but there are two easy ways of making it more inviting: the first is to take off all way by *heaving to*; the second takes off most of her way by *steering shy*.

Heaving to   When a sloop is hove to she is stopped in the water by her foresail being sheeted 'aback', on the windward side. The mainsail is left drawing to leeward, either close-hauled or with an eased sheet, and the whole equilibrium is balanced by the helm which is lashed so as to try to turn the boat into the wind.

A yacht with a traditional hull-form featuring a deep forefoot will maintain herself hove to with the wind well forward of the beam; indeed, a classic gaff cutter will normally take up what is virtually a close-hauled attitude. The more up-to-date hull-forms generally heave to with their bows further off the wind, but by juggling the

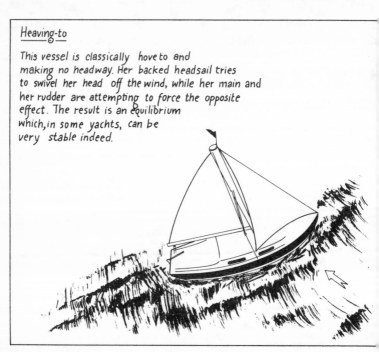

Heaving-to

This vessel is classically hove to and making no headway. Her backed headsail tries to swivel her head off the wind, while her main and her rudder are attempting to force the opposite effect. The result is an equilibrium which, in some yachts, can be very stable indeed.

sheets and tiller they can often be persuaded to improve their act. If the weather jib sheet is eased, the boat heads up; if the main is eased, she will fall off, pushed 'down' by the power of the headsail. The boat is balancing around her pivot point (Chapter 1) and her attitude can be adjusted more or less to suit the needs of the occasion.

Apparently, then, heaving to in order to reef is the ideal answer. Once she is hove to the boat requires no helmsman, so an extra hand is released to assist at the mast, or to put the reef in alone if there is no one else on watch. With the traditional hull-form the system worked wonderfully well. Many modern fin-keelers, however, are so delicately balanced about their centres of lateral resistance that when the mainsheet is eased to pull down the reef, the equilibrium is badly disturbed and the boat falls right off the wind. If a boat does not do this, then heaving to is the easiest way for her to encourage the crew to shorten down in good time, rather than hope the job will go away until it is too late.

By far the simplest way to put a yacht into the hove to state is to tack her, but instead of releasing the lee jib sheet as she comes to the wind, leaving it made fast. As the boat falls on to the new tack she will first try to spin on her heel, then, as you push the tiller down to leeward, she will make her peace with the situation and come to a standstill.

Heaving-to by tacking

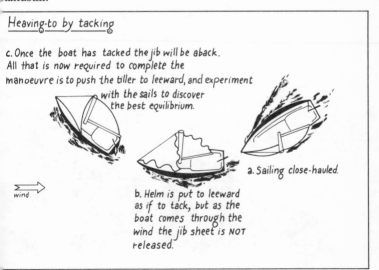

c. Once the boat has tacked the jib will be aback. All that is now required to complete the manoeuvre is to push the tiller to leeward, and experiment with the sails to discover the best equilibrium.

a. Sailing close-hauled.

wind

b. Helm is put to leeward as if to tack, but as the boat comes through the wind the jib sheet is NOT released.

If you feel your crew could use the exercise, you can of course winch the jib across to the windward side while the boat is sailing her course, then move the helm down as she begins to fall off the wind. She will heave to all right, but the winch-men won't like the way you've done it.

The amount of leeway a boat makes when she is hove to varies enormously according to her type, but it is important to consider in the context of this chapter the effect of a genoa. Basically, heaving to with a genoa set on a masthead rig is a wash-out. The sail will come aback against the spreaders where it is immediately at risk of damage. It will also overpower the effect of the mainsail, rendering the desired balance almost unobtainable. The effect of a genoa on a fractional rig is less undesirable, but even so it may prove too much for a satisfactory balance to be achieved.

With either masthead or fractional rigs, creative use of a roller genoa gives you an ideal opportunity to balance the boat when she is hove to.

In a modern yacht, heaving to is usually most useful when the boat is already under short sail, and you are going for the second or third reef. By then, you may well have a working jib set, under which she should heave to happily.

Steering shy Any boat, at any time, can be restrained in her exuberance by this simple expedient. The sheets are eased and the boat is

'Steering shy' to slow down boat

Sheets are eased and the boat is steered somewhat 'above' her course. With care, this can reduce speed to the slowest that conditions will allow, so as to make the foredeck a friendlier place.

wind

steered sufficiently above her course to spill wind out of the sails. How much wind you choose to dump will depend on conditions. If there is a lumpy sea running you'll need a certain amount of way on in order to retain control. If the water is flatter, you'll almost be able to stop, but it is vital that the boat be kept moving just above stalling speed. If she stalls, her head will fall off the wind despite your best efforts, and to allow this to happen when the hands are half-way through reefing is downright insensitive. You'll know when she is about to stall because the wheel or tiller will go 'spongy', and she will suddenly develop lee helm.

Running off for headsail changes   Either of the techniques we have just discussed is also useful when changing a headsail, but you'll have to bear in mind that if you are hove to, the boat will luff as soon as the jib comes down. Nevertheless, heaving to makes that initial journey to the plunging foredeck a great deal less fraught with anguish than would otherwise be the case.

Another way of keeping the acid level down for a headsail change is to run the boat dead down-wind for a few seconds while the crew work their way forward to drop the sail. The difference in the conditions on the deck of a boat going to windward and one running off is indescribable. Once the sail is on the deck, the yacht can be brought

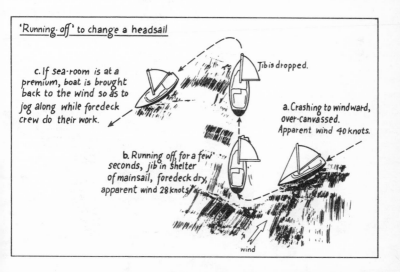

'Running-off' to change a headsail

c. If sea-room is at a premium, boat is brought back to the wind so as to jog along while foredeck crew do their work.

Jib is dropped.

a. Crashing to windward, over-canvassed. Apparent wind 40 knots.

b. Running off for a few seconds, jib in shelter of mainsail, foredeck dry, apparent wind 28 knots.

wind

back to the wind again if you are concerned about giving away your weather gauge.

The only danger attached to this method is that the crew are at risk from the clew of the genoa as it flogs from side to side, unable to decide whether to goose-wing itself or not. The problem can be nullified if you close-haul the monster in the lee of the mainsail. The job won't require any effort on the sheet-winch, and you gain the additional benefit of persuading the sail to drop on deck, safely inside the guardrails.

The question of which sail combination should be carried when the main is reefed and the Number One genoa is back in the locker is best decided by paying attention to the balance of the helm. The boat should be set up so that when she is sailing close to the wind she carries just a touch of weather helm. If she is given too much 'grunt up front', she may fall off to leeward at every pitch, while if her headsail is too small for the area of mainsail and/or mizzen on display, the helmsman may pass his day with the tiller round the back of his neck.

Let the boat talk to you, and give her what she wants. She knows better than you do what that should be, in order to let her go.

CHAPTER FIVE

Helming Under Sail

One of the exercises recommended by the Royal Yachting Association training scheme for dinghy sailors is called 'Rudderless Sailing'. The student lays his rudder in the bottom of the boat and proceeds to experiment with sail balance and the effects of induced heel until sufficient mastery has been achieved to sail the boat upwind, downwind and on a reach. Before the student is considered competent he must also tack and gybe.

Once you can do this, you can start to call yourself a sailor.

Such manoeuvres would be a very different proposition in a cruising yacht because of the impossibility of persuading her to heel to windward when required. However, the attitude engendered by the exercise should always remain uppermost in a skipper's mind: the rudder is only a part of the overall system for pointing the boat in the desired direction. If everything else is working in harmony, and the vessel is not being driven hard, a minimum of helm movement should suffice to keep her on the straight and narrow.

A skilled helmsman will be able to reduce even this amount of deflection of the rudder by thoughtful anticipation of the yacht's next move. With practice, this ends up as a deep-seated instinct which corrects the boat's wandering tendencies before they have begun. Such a person will keep a wheel-steered boat reaching in a straight line for the whole of a 2-hour trick and never move the helm more than a couple of spokes, which will please the boat mightily. Any excess movement of the rudder slows the yacht down, so it pays to concentrate on learning to feel what she is about. That way you don't fight her, and you please both yourself and her.

STEERING TO WINDWARD

In the days of gaff-rigged yachts with long bowsprits and even longer keels, the business of steering to windward was a matter of art and feeling. For much of the time you simply could not see the luff of the jib, so you set the boat in her groove by watching the true wind direction on the water, and by feeling through the seat of your fearnaught trousers. Today, in a well-tuned cruising yacht it is possible to learn in a week what used to take years because, from the outset, the boat can be sailed accurately to windward by the tell-tales on the jib luff.

Once the rig is set up to the skipper's satisfaction the responsibility for presenting it at the best angle to the flowing air rests with the helmsman. As a general proposition the tell-tales on both sides of the jib should be streaming smoothly aft, though in smooth water or strong wind, it may be acceptable to steer so 'high' that the *windward* ones flick upwards from time to time. The amount that this can be allowed depends on the power available from the rig and on how much the seas are stopping the boat. The feel of the helm and the speed of the boat supply the answer. If she slows too much her leeway will increase and any apparent gain from pointing high will be nullified.

Often, when the sail combination is just right for the average wind strength, the boat will be struggling in the gusts. When this happens, you can luff her gently so that those windward tell-tales kick up. This will indicate that the rig is ditching some of its power, and you will feel the boat come upright. So long as you don't overdo it there will be ample drive left to hammer through the squall, gaining rather than losing ground.

This technique is crucial when sailing a modern boat with a flat midships section and a deep fin keel. These yachts cannot be allowed to heel excessively, and constant vigilance is required to 'keep them on their feet.'

At no time when the apparent wind is forward of the beam, but particularly when close-hauled, should the *leeward* tell-tales be allowed to go dancing. The instant they do, the sails are seen to be stalling, which means she is being steered too far off the wind. She is not only giving away ground made good, she is also probably heeling far more

Steering to windward in waves

The technique of luffing to the crests and bearing away over the top is well worth practising. If executed to perfection, in a boat that is quick on the helm, it will reduce pounding to a minimum while producing the best possible speed to windward the circumstances can allow.

than she need be. The solution is to luff steadily until the situation is rectified.

Steering in waves When a boat which is quick on the helm (see Chapter 1) is being worked to windward in a seaway it pays dividends to steer her over the waves in order to stop her pounding. The technique is simple to describe, but it takes practice to develop the necessary feel to work it to perfection.

While the boat approaches the crest of a wave, she is steadily luffed above her proper course. As she traverses the crest, the helm is brought 'up' sharply so that she bears away down the back of the wave rather than falling headlong into the trough and crashing to a teeth-rattling near standstill. And so on. Once this process has been mastered, the right sort of yacht can be 'pumped' rhythmically to windward, making for a measurable improvement over the efforts of a similar boat that is sailing in a straight line. The negative results of the extra helm activity and the short periods when the rig is not presented ideally to the airstream are more than compensated for by the way the yacht is negotiating the waves.

Any attempt to do this in a heavy displacement, long-keeled yacht will be a total waste of time, but fortunately vessels of this type do not make such demands on their helmsmen. They are reluctant to pound in the first place, and even if they do occasionally drop off a steep wave, their displacement and easy sections carry them bravely through. The best way to work such a boat to windward in an awkward sea is to ease the sheets a touch and steer a few degrees off. The additional power created will be more than enough to do the business.

STEERING A ROLLING BOAT

In the last chapter we have seen how, as a boat rolls, she is subjected to forces which alternately induce her to round up, then to bear away. In hard conditions either of these can result in a broach which may have disastrous consequences if the yacht is heavily canvassed and being driven hard.

As she rolls to leeward the necessary weather helm to stop her luffing must be applied, then, as the motion carries the masthead to windward, a helping of lee helm will be required to prevent the dreaded gybe-broach.

A considerable degree of confidence is needed to do this well, especially to hold the tiller down to the lee side of the cockpit as the boat makes to roll over on top of you, but if the job is skilfully done, not only will the yacht sail straighter, she will also roll less. If, on the other hand, she is allowed to indulge herself, the rolling may increase rhythmically until there is nothing you can do to prevent a broach.

The good helmsman does all this by feel. As the stern lifts to ride down a wave he or she can tell which way the boat will try to roll and go. The corrective measure will be applied before the dive off course begins, and the rest of the crew will never know how well the job is being handled until they try it themselves. Because it is done by feel, it works just as well in the dark.

As in all questions of co-ordination, some are born more able at down-wind steering than others, but everyone is better for having practised, tiller in hand, listening with all their senses to what the boat is saying.

STEERING THROUGH A TACK

The process of going about on a fore-and-aft rigged yacht should be smooth, well drilled, and executed with a minimum of hard labour. It is ironic that this is usually the case on a well-run racing boat where there is any amount of muscle lying around the deck, as well as big winches to whip in the headsail sheet in a trice.

The fact that the cockpit gorillas hardly need to flex their biceps is due mainly to the quality of the helmsman. If he is skilled the boat will be brought quickly to the wind and quickly through it, so that the sails are kicking for a minimum of time, but once past the wind's eye the boat will be held a trifle high of the new tack for the few seconds it takes to grind in the headsail sheet. As soon as the sheet is home, the boat bears away on to a close-hauled heading and fills her sails. If the whole crew gets it right, the 90° turn will appear as a clean curve.

The converse of this ideal piece of teamwork occurs when the driver is so thrilled to have contrived to steer through the wind that he promptly falls off on to a beam reach, leaving his winch-grinders sweating and cursing. As he wanders around looking for the close-hauled groove, the long-suffering manual workers wind in the yards of flogging jib sheet which their leader has thoughtlessly donated to their cause.

Think about the folks in front of you when you're helming through a tack. If you give them a chance the tack will be faster as well as kinder to all concerned.

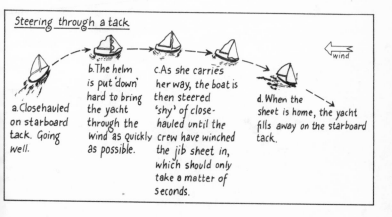

Steering through a tack

a. Closehauled on starboard tack. Going well.

b. The helm is put 'down' hard to bring the yacht through the wind as quickly as possible.

c. As she carries her way, the boat is then steered 'shy' of close-hauled until the crew have winched the jib sheet in, which should only take a matter of seconds.

d. When the sheet is home, the yacht fills away on the starboard tack.

wind

STEERING THROUGH A GYBE

Over the years the business of gybing has received more than its share of bad press, for no other reason than that if it is carried out carelessly or by accident in a strong breeze, damage to gear or bodies may result from the untamed anger of the boom.

Accidental gybes are best avoided by rigging a strong preventer any time it seems necessary. The way to gybe successfully is as follows:

* Steer almost dead down-wind, taking care to keep the boat moving straight.
* Sheet the mainsail hard in amidships *and make fast*, at least with a round turn, if there is no jamming cleat in the system. In a small, tiller-steered boat, the helmsman can do this himself, steering with his knees while he hauls in the sheet.
* Steer carefully through the gybe, making sure that the boat turns just far enough for the mainsail to flop across *and no further*. As the boom comes over, the yacht will tend to luff hard, so you'll have to be ready for it by giving the helm a firm preventive pull.
* As soon as the situation is well in hand (a matter of a couple of seconds only), the sheet is surged out and the new course taken up.
* If the boat is of extreme design, it may be necessary to let the mainsheet run as soon as the boom has come across, in order to control the boat's tendency to round up.

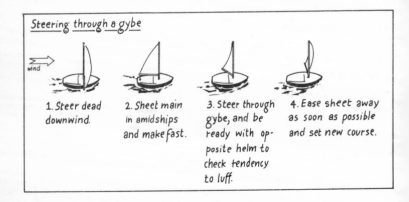

Steering through a gybe

wind

1. *Steer dead downwind.*

2. *Sheet main in amidships and make fast.*

3. *Steer through gybe, and be ready with opposite helm to check tendency to luff.*

4. *Ease sheet away as soon as possible and set new course.*

* On any boat which has a mainsheet traveller operated by lines, both ends must be made fast before gybing. The potential for traveller cars to gobble fingers is too great, and is ignored at your peril.

USE OF SHEETS TO ASSIST COURSE ALTERATIONS

Bearing away The greatest enlightenment offered to the observer about whether or not someone can sail a boat is what he does when he bears away. Either the mainsheet is instinctively eased as the helm goes up, or it isn't. The mediocre boat handler will heave the tiller to windward, forcing the boat against her will to turn off the wind. Once her new course is established he will trim the sails. The good skipper on the other hand eases the main as the helm comes up; the boat ceases to heel and all drive is removed from abaft her centre of lateral resistance so that she does not try to resist the turn. How can anyone be so brutish as to ask a yacht to fight all the laws which govern her actions?

It beats me.

When she's moving slowly, these effects are even more pronounced because the rudder is working poorly, if at all.

At any time, but particularly when the boat is stalled, she can be persuaded to bear away more positively by sheeting in the jib and ditching the mainsheet.

Luffing up When a boat is moving well, there is rarely a problem persuading her to luff closer to the wind. If the helm is released, she'll find her own way there, given time. However, as she comes up it is important to keep sheeting in the main, so that there is a continuing source of drive from abaft the centre of lateral resistance.

When a boat is being tacked from a reach to a reach, rather than close-hauled, this is even more important. If there is a strong wind and steep sea, a boat whose mainsheet is ignored may refuse to tack at all.

If the boat is almost, or completely stationary, she can only be made to head up by letting the jib right off and hauling in the mainsheet.

Backing the headsail Sometimes a yacht experiences problems in

45

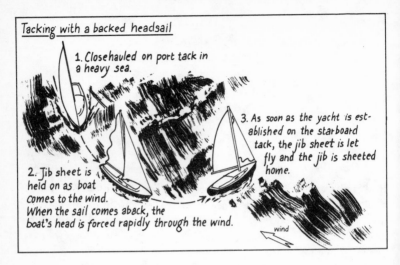

Tacking with a backed headsail

1. Closehauled on port tack in a heavy sea.

3. As soon as the yacht is established on the starboard tack, the jib sheet is let fly and the jib is sheeted home.

2. Jib sheet is held on as boat comes to the wind. When the sail comes aback, the boat's head is forced rapidly through the wind.

wind

forcing her head through the wind. This should never happen when she is being sailed properly unless conditions are unusually bad, but if it does, you can always persuade her to complete the manoeuvre by holding the jib sheet instead of releasing it as the sail begins to lift then flog. Once the boat is head to wind, the sail will fill in the aback position and the ship's head will be pushed across rapidly. As soon as you're sure she is through, release the sheet and haul it in on the 'new' side.

This technique is often useful in tight corners, but you should always remember that it may take off the last of the boat's way. When this happens, it becomes necessary to reverse the helm because the boat will soon be moving astern. Watch her carefully when you back the jib. If you get it wrong you may cover considerable ground astern before the boat decides to turn on to one tack or the other.

CHAPTER SIX

Slowing Down

In this chapter we'll concentrate on the delicate art of taking way off a boat and sailing her slowly. We have looked at the basic theory of how a boat works and we've considered some of the skills which are used to help her to go fast. There is now enough information on board to begin looking at the real business of boat handling. Later on in the book we will sort out the most common day-to-day manoeuvres, but for the moment we'll deal with the various available methods of ditching power from the rig without having the yacht blow around like a leaf in the wind.

The close reach So long as you can plan your strategy to allow the boat to approach an objective on a close reach, you have the ideal circumstance for controlling your speed. If she is sailing at about 60° from the true wind she can be progressively slowed down by easing

The close reach
By spilling a measured amount of wind, speed on a close reach can be controlled to a nicety.

wind

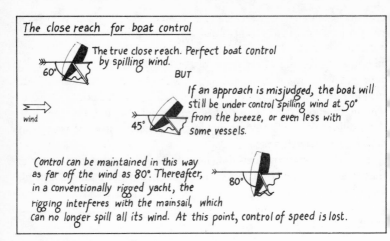

The close reach for boat control

The true close reach. Perfect boat control by spilling wind.

60°

wind

BUT

If an approach is misjudged, the boat will still be under control spilling wind at 50° from the breeze, or even less with some vessels.

45°

Control can be maintained in this way as far off the wind as 80°. Thereafter, in a conventionally rigged yacht, the rigging interferes with the mainsail, which can no longer spill all its wind. At this point, control of speed is lost.

80°

sheets to spill wind. Even if you have misjudged matters so that you need to bear away a few degrees it will not make much difference because it is possible to spill wind from most mainsails on any heading of up to 75° from the wind's eye. On the other hand, if your situation requires you to haul up a little to windward, you have still 15° to go from your 60° before the boat is close-hauled. By then the forward component of her sail power will be so weak that if some of it is given away by wind-spilling, the boat will rapidly stall and make leeway from which nothing but a tack or two will extricate her. In order to avoid this you need only to keep the wind at least 50° on the bow, and all will be well.

If the boat's speed falls so low while close-reaching that she begins to stall, you'll know straight away because she will develop lee helm. To correct her you haul in the mainsheet; as the sail begins to bite, the extra area drawing abaft the pivot point will neutralize the helm and the boat will move gently ahead again. When there is a sea running and more drive is required to retain the keel's grip on the water, this can be achieved by letting draw a part of the jib as well. Bring both main and jib sheets on until the leeches of the sails are filling sufficiently to keep the boat moving sweetly.

You cannot beat a close reach for control, but unfortunately life is such that a boat must frequently be asked to lose way in circumstances which do not allow her that luxury. Suppose you are entering a crowded anchorage downwind on a blustery day. The last thing you want is to come blazing in at 7½ knots, gybing through the boats like a demoniac skier attempting the giant slalom with a head full of drink. In a tideway you are often prevented by the stream from approaching your mooring or an alongside berth with the wind forward of the beam. There may also be times as you sail up a peaceful river when you might want to dawdle for no better reason than to enjoy the view.

On all these and many other occasions, the question of taking off way *down-wind* will arise.

The overriding consideration on a conventionally rigged yacht is that as soon as the wind moves abaft the beam the mainsail can no longer spill wind because it is pressed against the shrouds. Control of speed is therefore lost. The obvious solution is to drop the main and proceed under headsail alone, since headsails can be 'feathered' at any wind angle. Sometimes, however, it is useful to be able to leave the main hoisted, but to reduce its drive.

Stalling the main provides a reasonable method of spoiling the sail's efficiency. If the wind is on the quarter and you sheet it hard in, it will no longer function as an aerofoil. It will still shove the boat along by virtue of its area alone, but its power will be much diminished.

With the wind right aft, a main sheeted on to the centre-line of the boat creates very little push, yet is still there if you need it a few minutes later.

Scandalizing This is an even more effective means of achieving the desired result. The centre boom-vang is disconnected from the boom, the mainsheet is overhauled to its stopper knot, and the boom end is hoisted as high as it can go by hauling away on the topping-lift. If your boat has a long enough mainsheet the effect of all this is most gratifying. The sail flops around not knowing quite what to do, until the lift is released and the power is called up again by pulling in the sheet.

The art of scandalizing was even more effective in the days of gaff mainsails. The boom of the sail was topped a foot or two and the peak halyards were eased away, instantly reducing sail area by half. If a complete result was looked for, a loose-footed sail could then be made to disappear utterly by tricing the tack up almost as far as the gaff-jaws.

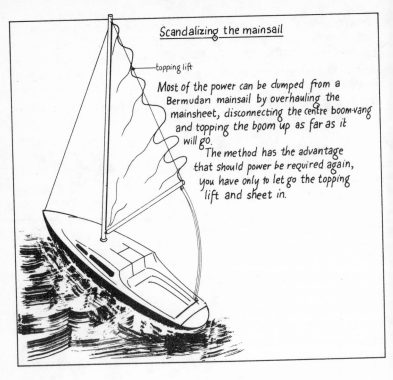

Scandalizing the mainsail

topping lift

Most of the power can be dumped from a
Bermudan mainsail by overhauling the
mainsheet, disconnecting the centre boom-vang
and topping the boom up as far as it
will go.
The method has the advantage
that should power be required again,
you have only to let go the topping
lift and sheet in.

If the boat is moving slowly off the wind and she has genuinely
finished with her mainsail, the best thing is to drop it, stow it, and
forget it. The manoeuvre can then be completed under headsail alone,
controlling speed by spilling wind, as usual.

The biggest problem you are likely to encounter now is that in a
strongish breeze the windage of a flogging genoa may provide sufficient push to keep the yacht trundling along at 2 or 3 knots. This
may be faster than you want to go if you are hoping to pick up a
mooring or come alongside. The only answer to this is to drop the
headsail as well and 'blow' along under bare poles. If you are still
carrying too much way for your taste, there is not a lot more that you
can do about it, short of throwing a bucket over the stern. If your
speed should fall too low, you can hoist a few feet of genoa and hold
the leech out by hand to catch as much or as little wind as you want.

The boat with a roller headsail of course has no such problems.
Perfect down-wind speed control is available at a heave of the furling

line; no flogging sails; no scrambling around over slippery heaps of canvas on the foredeck to do the human jib-sheet act; in fact, nothing to laugh at at all. The roller-furling genoa may leave something to be desired in terms of set when deeply reefed, but as a boat-handling tool it is without peer. It also gives the helmsman a clear view under the foot of the jib of the various obstacles that have to be avoided in a crowded anchorage.

AND STOPPING...

Just like a motor vehicle that is thrown out of gear, a sailing boat luffed head to wind will keep on moving under the impetus of her own momentum until this is exhausted. However, unlike a road vehicle, or to a lesser extent a vessel under power, the sailing boat has no brakes. She will carry her way until the wind resistance of her flogging sails and her topsides, coupled with her skin friction dragging through the water, combine to snuff it out.

It is vital to understand how far your boat carries her way under varying circumstances. Without this knowledge, all manoeuvres under sail are doomed to failure, and it is lack of confidence in this matter which, more than any other subject, causes people to fight shy of *sailing* their boats.

The working boatman in the days of sail planned all his movements in harbour with this in his mind. His whole way of thinking revolved around it. He probably even luffed up to his garden gate as he walked home for his tea. And he never in his life drove a wheeled vehicle with brakes. Because of this, the boat-handling section of his mind was not polluted in the way that ours is. We assume that in some mysterious way it is our right to be able to apply the brakes when things don't go as we'd hoped. We organize all our comings and goings with brakes in mind, and so we fire up our engines outside the harbour wall and drop our sails. This relieves us of the need for planning which was the essence of the traditional boatman's day. With an engine running we can proceed straight into the wind's eye and we can, within reason, stop at any time and at any angle to the wind. The need rapidly to assess a situation on the two premises that the boat cannot sail better than 50° to the wind, and can only be stopped by the running down of her own momentum or some smart line handling, is thus removed. Unfortunately, a tremendous amount of job satisfaction goes out the port-hole with it.

It is too easy to rationalize our own shyness and to demean the achievements of our forebears with remarks such as, 'Ah, but you see, the seas and the harbours were less crowded in *their* day.'

Nonsense! Check out one of those old postcards depicting 'Anstruther. The herring fleet comes in. 1898'. Wall-to-wall sailing vessels is what we see. Furthermore, they are not short-keeled modern Bermudan sloops which tack instantly through 90° and which carry their way for 20–30yds. Those are 40-ton luggers, needing a crew of 10 to go about, and moving inexorably ahead for the length of a football pitch and more when luffed from a 6-knot reach.

To handle a boat under sail, we need to rethink some of our entrenched attitudes; we need above all things to understand about carrying way.

How any boat will behave can only be determined by experiment (see Chapter 7), but it is possible to make a good guess by considering her hull-form. If she is a heavy-displacement craft, she will go a lot further than will a lightweight boat of the same length. Similarly, a 35-ft fishing smack packed with inside ballast will still be moving sedately ahead through a cross-wind long after a flat-floored racing yacht half her length again has begun to blow sideways.

Once committed to a head-to-wind standstill a sailing yacht ceases to be under proper command. She cannot stay head to wind for any time at all unless her bow is tethered to something. The will to do so is just not in her, and she will fall off on to one tack or the other. If you're quick you can generally dictate which tack this will be, but even so, the boat will have to sail off down-wind then beat back up again if she is to regain the position at which she stopped. It is therefore important to *keep way on* until you have arrived at the point where the boat is either to be anchored, or secured to a dock or a mooring buoy.

If the boat does lose all way while head to wind before you are ready for her, she can be induced to fall on to the best tack for the circumstances by moving the helm so that the rudder points in the direction you want the stern to go. As she moves astern under the influence of the wind, the rudder will help kick her around. The job can be completed by backing the jib on to the same side as the rudder.

If both these actions are taken just as the boat loses the last of her way, and not a moment sooner, she will spin round and a happy recovery is assured. If you take action too late, the tack she adopts will be a lottery, since once she has started to swing, there will be little you can do to stop her.

The heart of every successful manoeuvre is planning and anticipation. Think yourself back into the mind of those men who had never used a wheel in anger, and retain a grip on your destiny by keeping the boat in a usable position relative to the wind for as long as it takes to work her sweetly to a standstill, just where you want her.

CHAPTER SEVEN

Sizing Up the Scene

Before considering any manoeuvre under either power or sail, a correct assessment of what the wind is doing is required. It is also axiomatic that the tidal stream (or any other current) be correctly judged.

True and apparent wind   The *true wind* is the breeze that is blowing across the deck of a vessel which is stationary relative to the ground. As soon as she begins to move, the effect of her passage through the airstream alters its apparent strength and direction. The resultant, or *apparent wind* may be significantly different from the true wind. Sails are set to the apparent wind which is blowing past them, but when planning your strategy it is usual to refer to the true wind, because this will decide such crucial questions as whether a buoy or

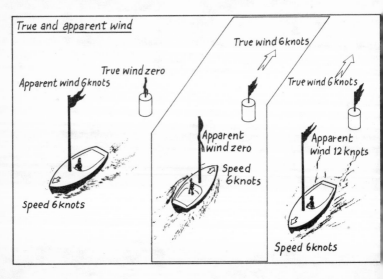

harbour entrance can be laid on the next tack, or whether it will be necessary to gybe at the next bend in the river.

A useful way to ponder the mystery of apparent wind is to consider an angler in a small motor-driven boat. He begins his day on a mooring buoy in a flat calm with his flag hanging limply from its staff. As he motors off at 6 knots through the still air, his passage creates an apparent headwind of 6 knots. Later in the day, back on his buoy, a light 6-knot breeze has kicked in. The angler decides he will motor in a down-wind direction at 6 knots in search of a better catch. In no time he has 'caught up the wind'. The air is flowing at 6 knots and he is motoring through the water at the same speed in the same direction. This means that his boat is no longer moving relative to the airstream, so the resulting apparent wind across his flag is zero.

If he gets sick of this and decides to head back for his mooring he will need to put on a sweater because he will now be logging 6 knots straight into a true wind of 6 knots. The natural headwind of his own progress will add to the true wind to create an apparent headwind of 12 knots.

Suppose he now veers off at 90° to the true wind, what happens then? His flag makes a compromise between the two winds which it thinks are blowing. It is aware of the 6-knot headwind of the angler's motion, but it also feels the 6-knot true wind from directly abeam. The apparent wind is the resultant of these two. It will be coming from 45° on the bow at about 8½ knots.

Whenever a boat is moving ahead, her apparent wind is always blowing from closer to her bow than is the true wind. The only exception is when the true wind is dead aft. Then, the speed of the boat's progress over the ground will diminish the apparent wind, while the direction of both remains unchanged.

Wind assessment   When a vessel is in motion, under either sail or power, the wind which your senses (with the exception of your sight) pick up is the apparent wind. The same is true of any instruments the boat may have, unless she has a computer feeding on not only wind instruments, but also the ship's log. Even this will not give a strictly correct answer unless it is programmed to consider information about the tidal stream, which also affects apparent wind.

The apparent wind direction can be judged by reference to a burgee or a 'windex'. It can also be very finely ascertained by feeling it as it blows over your ears. Face the wind, and carefully turn your head a few degrees from side to side, until you are sure that both ears are sensing the same amount of breeze. This method is extremely accurate, but if all else fails, there is always the good old wet finger held optimistically aloft.

These methods also hold for sorting out the true wind direction when the boat is alongside the dock and going nowhere, but if you favour the electronic approach to nature you'll have to remember to switch off your computer at this point. If the tide is flowing past a through-hull log impeller, the computer will think the boat is moving at that speed relative to the breeze and will make corrections to what it thinks is the apparent wind. You'll just have to educate the thing by using the 'off' switch.

So far, so good. But how do you sort out the true wind from the apparent when the boat is under way? In the absence of the computer (and when it comes to boat handling, the beast won't help you one jot) there are but two answers to this: the first is to make an informed guess based on the fact that the true wind will be further aft than the burgee and your ear-lobes are suggesting; the second, and by far the more accurate method, is to use your eyes. There may be flags, smoke, etc. ashore, but compared with the gospel, these are as broken reeds. The place to see the true wind is *on the water*. Never mind the waves, look for the small, dark wind ripples. Unless it is really blowing these are rarely above an inch high, but they are always visible, just as they are in a bowl of over-warm soup across which a well-mannered diner is surreptitiously blowing. Like the gourmet's cooling breath on the consommé, the wind on the sea is blowing at right angles to the ripples, and a right angle is easy to construct in the mind's eye. Don't look at the waves. They may be affected by many strange forces; focus your gaze on the tiny ripples, and all will be revealed.

For some reason, many people find these blatant little signposts difficult to spot at first. Some see them straight away, others don't, but once they are isolated from the rest of the visual data being pumped into the brain they provide the answer to the question of true wind direction. So if you don't find them obvious to start with, it is worth persevering.

Currents and tidal streams The only way to assess the direction of tide or current is to watch the water relative to some fixed object, uch as a river bank or a buoy. It's not unknown for a student skipper who has just received an overdose of class-room theory to reply, when asked which way the tide is running past the dock to which he is moored, 'Hang on, I'll just check the time of high water!'

Obviously this is nonsense. Apart from anything else, the tide tables are at best merely predictions which may differ on the day from the facts, but even if they were 'bomb-proof' it would still be a total waste of time to consult them.

Look over the side. Spit in the water if necessary. That's all that's required.

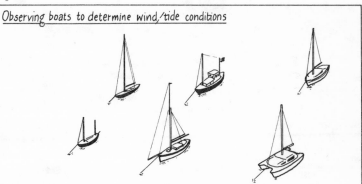

Observing boats to determine wind/tide conditions

1. These boats indicate that either there is no appreciable current, or if there is one, that it is running WITH the wind.

2. The fact that all the boats are lying across the wind indicates that they are head-up to a fairly strong current.

3. This situation tells you that wind and current are in opposition, and that the current is relatively weak. The deep-draft cutter is probably lying to the stream, while the light-weight catamaran is obviously wind-rode.

If you're approaching a stretch of water where the current is an unknown quantity from your present position, much can be learned from observing the lie of any moored or anchored vessels. Are they wind-rode? If so, there is either no stream or, if there is one, it's running with the wind or is too weak to overcome the effect of the tidal stream. When the boats are not lying to the breeze, there is evidence of a current of some sort. Should every vessel be 'head up' to the same direction, the stream is positively identified. If there is some discrepancy, this may be accounted for by the different hull-forms of the boats. Deep, long-keeled boats will lie almost exclusively to the tide, except in strong cross-winds. Shallow craft such as catamarans or bilge-keel yachts may well find themselves athwart the tide, and so on. An informed guess will give you enough information to rough out a plan of action.

Occasionally you'll be about to come alongside a dock on the bank of a river around the turn of the tide. Try as you may you cannot judge or observe which way, if any, the stream is moving, but you don't want to risk coming down-tide on to the dock. When this state of affairs is upon you the only thing to do is get the boat moving slowly, then steer her straight across the river towards the dock for a few seconds. She will be across any tide that is moving, and you'll be able to see what is going on. Watch out for eddies close inshore running in a contrary direction to the main stream.

The up-tide approach Whenever a boat is being brought to a standstill 'over the ground' where a current of any strength is running, it is of primary importance that, regardless of any considerations involving the wind, she approaches her mark *head to tide*.

There are two reasons for this. The first is obvious: it is simplicity itself to stop a boat when she is going up-current. Stopping her when she has the tide behind her will be extremely tricky under power and technically impossible under sail. The second reason is more subtle and it is beautiful in its various spin-offs. When a boat in a strong tide is stationary over the ground, either on a mooring, or because she is about to pick one up, she is *still moving ahead through the water*, and she can therefore be steered. This opens up all sorts of delights when coming alongside (Chapters 14 and 15), and if the knowledge is used properly, it makes mooring and anchoring far easier in a tideway than in slack water.

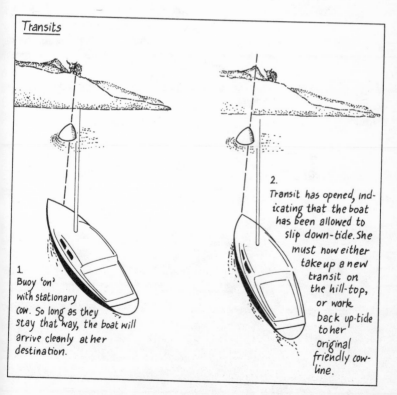

Transits

1. Buoy 'on' with stationary cow. So long as they stay that way, the boat will arrive cleanly at her destination.

2. Transit has opened, indicating that the boat has been allowed to slip down-tide. She must now either take up a new transit on the hill-top, or work back up-tide to her original friendly cow-line.

Use of transits in tidal manoeuvres Pre-judging the actual speed of a current is a nigh-on-impossible task. Fortunately, it is rarely necessary to do so because the boat can always be kept on line by using *transits*. Once you've decided which way you want the boat to travel over the ground for a particular part of a manoeuvre (usually the final approach), all you have to do is pick out any two fixed objects which line up behind your immediate destination. These will rarely be an 'official' transit; more often you will use a clump of grass on the river bank in line with a gap in the hill; or maybe it'll be a mooring bollard 'on' with a motor-car door handle, or the mooring buoy you are hoping to pick up transited with a distant cow lying in a field.

What you choose is unimportant, but if you try to keep a boat going straight without any such help, you're going to need the judgement of Nelson to be in with even a starter's chance. Use a transit though, and your arrival at the point you are aiming for is guaranteed. Absolutely no skill is required. If the selected objects start to hint that you are being set 'down', you steer more into the tide, power up the rig, or order up a few more revs. If they 'open' the other way you throttle back, let go the jib sheet, or steer a touch more across the tide. The transit will tell you every time whether or not you've got it right. What's more, unlike tide tables, computers fed with flawed data, or your own subjective assessment, they will never tell you a lie.

CHAPTER EIGHT

General Handling Under Power

The art of handling a single-screw vessel is not to be underestimated, particularly when she is a deep-keeled yacht with a tiny propeller and a large amount of top-hamper to catch the wind. The number of times one hears remarks such as, 'The old *Mud-gobbler*'s a great sea boat, but she's always been unpredictable under power', is nobody's business. Yet some people seem only to have to breathe on an awkward boat and she will perform miracles for them. She will slide sideways into an apparently impossible berth; she will take way off in a straight line; she will even steer astern.

Why?

What are the secrets to which these skippers are privy that lesser mortals never find? There is only really one, and it's called *prop-walk*. All the other tricks and techniques are merely an extension of boat handling under sail. Principles, such as stalling at low speeds in a cross-wind, the way the boat pivots about her centre of lateral resistance, and such like, remain unaltered. The only thing different is that the boat is being urged to move not by sails, whose balance can be juggled almost infinitely so long as you don't try to sail straight into the wind, but by a propeller, which is firmly sited somewhere in the vicinity of the rudder.

THE PADDLE-WHEEL EFFECT (PROP-WALK)

Because it is turning like a mill, a propeller does not deliver its push as a smooth-edged gush of water sluicing out directly astern of the boat. Instead, it sends out a vortex which not only drives the yacht ahead or astern, but also tends to push her stern to one side or the other.

When the vessel is making way in proper proportion to her engine

61

revolutions, the propeller munches satisfyingly through the water, and these sideways effects are minimized. If the propeller is ideally sited forward of and reasonably close to the rudder, they are unlikely to be noticeable at all, because the prop-wash will be running directly over the rudder blade, a tiny deflection of which at cruising speeds will be sufficient to neutralize them.

It is at the slow velocities required for close-quarters boat handling that prop-walk is most noticeable because until the yacht is moving well the propeller tends to thrash round without really grabbing the water. This aggravates its sideways tendencies, particularly when the engine is going astern, because propellers are designed to push boats ahead, and few do both jobs equally well.

Another problem about astern drive is that when the boat is not moving ahead, the rudder won't work very well either. If the engine is thrown ahead and the rudder blade is put hard over, the resulting gush of water to one side of the boat will force the stern to cartwheel around in the opposite direction, assuming the propeller is sited forward of the rudder, as is usually the case. No such benefits are available when going astern. The propeller is an inefficient shape, and ends up shooting an inordinate amount of water out to whichever side

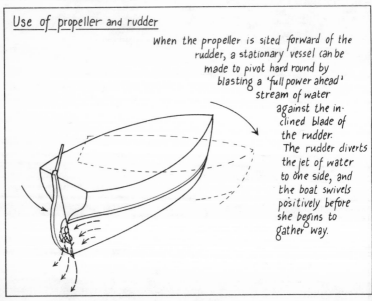

Use of propeller and rudder

When the propeller is sited forward of the rudder, a stationary vessel can be made to pivot hard round by blasting a 'full power ahead' stream of water against the inclined blade of the rudder. The rudder diverts the jet of water to one side, and the boat swivels positively before she begins to gather way.

of the boat its habit dictates. The rudder isn't much help, and the result is that heavy prop-walk is experienced.

Right- and left-handed propellers Most propellers are right-handed, which means that, looked at from aft, they turn clockwise when they are going ahead. What counts most to the skipper, though, is what is going to happen when he puts the engine astern.

In the case of the right-handed propeller, the stern will walk to port if the propeller is turning astern, and rather less to starboard when going ahead. A left-handed propeller will have the opposite effect.

The strength of 'propeller effects' varies greatly from boat to boat and depends on such things as keel form, rudder size and position, engine power, and the propeller itself. Generally speaking, if she has a reasonable-sized engine and a decent propeller, a modern yacht with fin keel and spade rudder will be far less affected than a deep-keeled vessel. Why this should be remains a mystery, but true it usually is.

Discovering prop-walk There are two ways to find out which way a boat is going to swing when the engine is put astern. The first method is useful if you are already under way and still don't know.

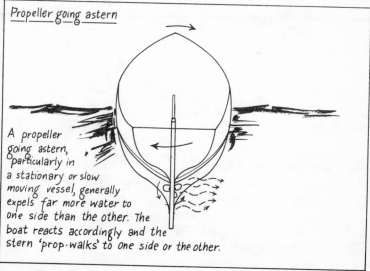

Propeller going astern

A propeller going astern, particularly in a stationary or slow moving vessel, generally expels far more water to one side than the other. The boat reacts accordingly and the stern 'prop-walks' to one side or the other.

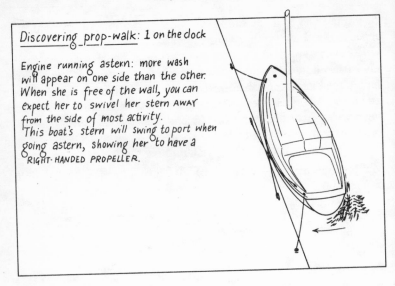

Discovering prop-walk: 1 on the dock

Engine running astern: more wash will appear on one side than the other. When she is free of the wall, you can expect her to swivel her stern AWAY from the side of most activity.
This boat's stern will swing to port when going astern, showing her to have a RIGHT-HANDED PROPELLER.

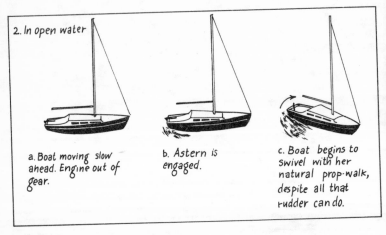

2. In open water

a. Boat moving slow ahead. Engine out of gear.

b. Astern is engaged.

c. Boat begins to swivel with her natural prop-walk, despite all that rudder can do.

Find yourself a stretch of calm water sheltered from any strong wind. If you can't escape the breeze, the exercise should be done with the boat motoring dead before the wind. Arrange for the boat to be moving slowly ahead with the engine out of gear. Now select astern and give the engine about half speed, making sure at the same time that you are steering firmly straight ahead. Watch the bow; in a few seconds you will see it slew to one side or the other. It will always be the same side, and the stern, of course, will be swinging in the opposite direction.

The second method has the benefit that it can be carried out while you are alongside. Start the engine, check the bow line and the stern spring, then put the engine one third astern. Look over each quarter. You'll see far more water welling up on one side than the other and you'll know that whenever you are going astern, your stern will try to swing away from the side with the greater disturbance.

Making use of prop-walk   Once you have established what your boat's natural preferences are, you will be unwise to ask her to do anything which is against her inclinations. Prop-walk is a powerful tool in the search for boat handling without blunders. If it is ignored a potentially pliable vessel can become a perfect incubus.

Coming Alongside   Whenever a boat is brought alongside under power, it is vital to consider which way she will swivel when you put the engine astern to stop her. If she has a right-handed propeller she is going to swing her stern to port. If all other things are equal you should lay her on the dock port-side to, so as to encourage her to tuck her stern in neatly.

The Short Turn   Sometimes you need to turn a yacht in less distance than her natural turning circle. Occasionally she must manage in little more than her own length. The fin-and-spade boat is often able to turn very tightly indeed by virtue of her large rudder and small lateral area. Boats with more of their hulls in the water may find greater difficulty. For them, the secret lies in using the prop-walk.

First, the boat is set up so that she is turning her favourite way, and has room enough to do so. The chosen spot is approached at a slow speed. When she has reached the right position, you put the helm hard over, and the boat begins to turn. Once she has gone as far as you are prepared to let her, the engine is put half astern *and the helm is left where it is*. The boat will continue to move slowly ahead but the stern will prop-walk around, tightening the turn considerably. After a few seconds, the boat will stop making any forward progress, but will carry on swivelling. This will continue as she starts to gather sternway. Most rudders will still be ineffectual, and if that is the case

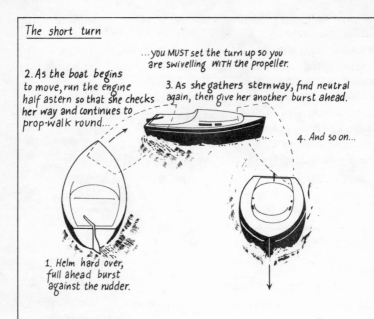

The short turn

...you MUST set the turn up so you are swivelling WITH the propeller.

2. As the boat begins to move, run the engine half astern so that she checks her way and continues to prop-walk round...

3. As she gathers sternway, find neutral again, then give her another burst ahead.

4. And so on...

1. Helm hard over, full ahead burst against the rudder.

The secret of turning in your own length is to use propeller and rudder, but never to let the boat gather way.

leave the helm where it is, but if the rudder is found to be working, reverse it.

Before the boat has travelled any distance astern put her out of gear again, make sure the helm is set so that she is steering into the turn once more, then put her hard ahead. When the jet of water hits the rudder, she will swivel round firmly, but the effect will diminish as she begins to make headway. As soon as you see her turn is widening, put her astern again. Keep up the sequence until you are around.

The question of how long the engine should be allowed to remain either ahead or astern during this manoeuvre can only be decided after experiment.

Making Sternway   Steering a boat astern under power can be a nightmare. Some boats (usually the fin-and-spade brigade) behave themselves perfectly, following obediently where their rudders are pointing. Others are unwilling, slow to catch on to what is required, and awkward when they do. A few are downright impossible.

What makes matters so difficult is that every boat has a certain critical speed astern, below which her rudder cannot overcome her prop-walk. Once you have found what this speed is, success is just a matter of knowing which way she will veer off, giving her room in which to do so, and then gritting your teeth and winding her up as quickly as you can. Control is usually established somewhere between 1 and 3 knots, but some boats can never go fast enough.

When your boat is making sternway, remember that the rudder is temporarily pivoted on the 'wrong edge' and can easily take charge. This may result in personal injury if you get in the way of the tiller; it can also damage the rudder pintles, and if it causes you to 'back up' into another yacht, it'll give you a nasty smack in the wallet. The only advice that can be offered is, 'If you're going to hit a row of yachts, always pick the cheapest.'

A yacht can often be helped to pull herself into line by giving her a sheer against the propeller before you start going astern. You can sometimes arrange this with lines if you are alongside, or by throwing the stern across with the rudder if you are manoeuvring freely. Half of her tendency to swing will then be taken up before she hits the straight line, so she'll only go half as far beyond it before you gain steerage way.

Another action which can help to minimize the unpleasantness is

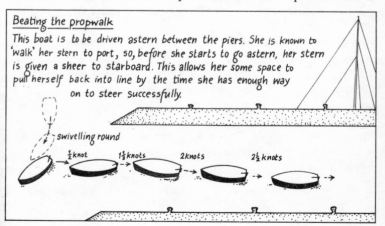

Beating the propwalk

This boat is to be driven astern between the piers. She is known to 'walk' her stern to port, so, before she starts to go astern, her stern is given a sheer to starboard. This allows her some space to pull herself back into line by the time she has enough way on to steer successfully.

swivelling round

½ knot   1½ knots   2 knots   2½ knots

to feed in the revs gradually. This avoids the thrashing propeller so productive of prop-walk, and helps the device to gain a grip on the water more rapidly. In the same vein, you can sometimes ease the situation while making sternway by throwing the engine out of gear for a while. This eliminates prop-walking altogether, and some boats will be ready to be steered back into line if it is done. Others, unfortunately, will remain unimpressed; once they've started to swing, it seems that nothing can stop them.

You'll only find out exactly where your own boat stands in this plethora of possibilities by experiment, but never forget that a sailing boat is highly unstable when she is under way astern. Propeller and rudder effects are only half the overall answer. On the day, windage might be just as important. If you are going to have to go astern in a cross-wind you'll need to assess whether the windage on your bows will add to, or subtract from, the boat's natural inclination to swivel one way.

There are other effects of the propeller about which it becomes increasingly difficult to generalize, but over which each and every boat will behave predictably, if individually. A typical example is what happens when a boat is moving ahead at 4 or 5 knots and you want to take way off by giving her a burst astern. Which side will her stern favour, if any? It may well be different to what you would expect. Once again, the answer can only be found by experiment.

There is enough theory below decks by now to tackle the business of boat handling in more practical terms. In the next chapter we will look at a series of exercises and experiments which can be essayed in the privacy of a quiet anchorage well out of harm's way. Once those are under your belt you'll have found out enough about your boat's behaviour to be able to approach any manoeuvre, fast or slow, in harbour or at sea, with complete confidence that you do at least know what's going on.

CHAPTER NINE

An Alternative Day's Yachting

There is absolutely nobody who can predict exactly what an unfamiliar boat will do in a given set of circumstances. An experienced skipper may be able to hazard a guess based on the boat's probable underwater shape, the power of her engine, the position of her masts, whether or not she sports a bowsprit, etc. but even he will need to experiment before he is sure.

Most professionals use a series of simple tests before laying a strange boat alongside a dock, particularly if she looks as though she may prove troublesome. In this chapter you will find a number of experiments that are useful in determining a vessel's behaviour. There are also some exercises which are designed to sharpen up individual skills and perceptions. These will be of use to those who, due to other pressures, cannot spend as much time sailing as they would like. If this is so in your case, it is well worth setting aside a day at the beginning of each season for no other purpose than to throw the boat around. It is a lot of fun, and it helps to free your mind from the fetters of that wretched motor-car which you drive every day of your life.

BOAT-HANDLING EXERCISES: UNDER POWER

Natural attitude   It is always useful to know what angle a boat will adopt to the wind when floating free in calm water. Most sloops will settle at about 140° from the wind. Once this has been ascertained you'll know how hard the boat is trying to blow off her course on slow-speed approaches with the breeze at various angles from the bow. The closer she is to her natural attitude, the less unstable she'll be.

Carrying way Try taking the power off at steady speeds of 2 knots, 3 knots and 5 knots and see how far she goes.

Stalling speed The best way to find out about this is to choose a windy day and a calm location. Motor straight into the wind, throw her out of gear, and see how far you can keep the boat moving before her head blows off to one side or the other. As soon as you begin to lose her, regain control with a burst of power against the rudder blade. How much power is needed, and for how long, to do no more than bring her back into line? This exercise is first-class for developing a feel for your boat.

Now do the same thing with the wind at varying angles from the bow. Again, what you're after is to feel the developing stall through the tiller or wheel as lee helm becomes apparent. Practise giving the boat as little power as you can to beat the stall.

Next time you're approaching a berth with the wind blowing hard on to it, you'll be glad you've been working at this question. Your problem will be to keep the boat's head up, while moving at the slowest possible speed, which is exactly what the exercise is about.

Prop-walk In the previous chapter we have looked at the two main methods of discovering which way your boat prop-walks. Once you've worked it out, try a few 360° short turns. Nearly all yachts will spin around in less than two boat's-lengths. Is yours open to persuasion?

Taking way off in a strong following wind One of the more obscure effects of prop-walk may crop up when you try to take way off the boat with a burst astern while she is carrying her way towards an objective. This is likely to occur when you are approaching a dock down-wind in a stiff breeze with no room to turn round and come in 'head up'. A light displacement yacht may blow down the breeze at 3 or 4 knots, and never stop at all. A heavier boat with more in the water will not be so unruly, but the same difficulty may still be experienced.

The odd thing is that above a certain speed the propeller effect may prove less drastic than you expect. It can even contrive to reverse itself. You could be expecting the stern to throw to port as you carefully feed on the astern-drive revs, when it suddenly veers off to starboard instead.

The reasons for this are deeply entrenched within the mysteries of laminar flow and cavitation, but for whatever reason it is happening, you don't want to discover it for the first time as you are approaching a narrow lock-gate with pricy gin-palaces stacked up each side of it.

Try the boat out on a windy day. Then try her again on another occasion under similar circumstances. The only guarantee is that she'll be predictable in her apparent unpredictability. If she isn't, there has been a subtle change in the conditions which you have not noticed.

Making sternway   As was the case with prop-walk, we've already considered the general 'ins and outs' of moving astern. The time to put it to the test is now, when there is plenty of room. Have a go up-wind first, so that the boat's greater windage forward will help keep

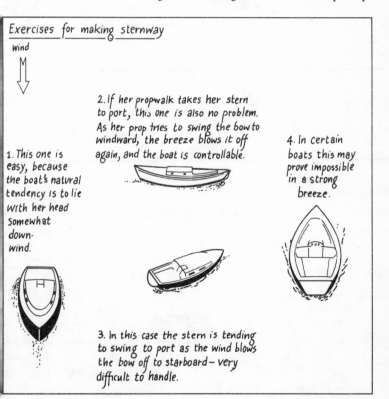

Exercises for making sternway

wind

1. This one is easy, because the boat's natural tendency is to lie with her head somewhat down-wind.

2. If her propwalk takes her stern to port, this one is also no problem. As her prop tries to swing the bow to windward, the breeze blows it off again, and the boat is controllable.

3. In this case the stern is tending to swing to port as the wind blows the bow off to starboard – very difficult to handle.

4. In certain boats this may prove impossible in a strong breeze.

her in a straight line. Then try it across the breeze 'against the propeller', then go in the opposite direction with the prop-walk helping to counteract the wind. Finally, see if she can be persuaded to go astern dead down-wind. If it is a fresh afternoon she won't like that at all, but at least you'll know whether or not it is possible.

If the whole business has gone smoothly, you could round off by attempting a figure-of-eight as a final *tour de force*.

UNDER SAIL

Close reaching and wind awareness   Once you have selected a sensible sail combination for the conditions, a good starting-point is to lay the boat beam-on to the wind and let off the sheets. See if she will lose way completely or if she continues to creep ahead. You may find that the leech of the mainsail will not spill the last of its wind; if so, release the centre vang. It will make a big difference.

If the boat still won't lose all her way beam-on, bring her steadily up towards the wind, and find out how close she must be before she will stop. That is the 'low' side of her 'close-reaching window'.

Now get her moving in this direction and sail her slowly, spilling wind all the time, ever higher until she just won't take any more. As

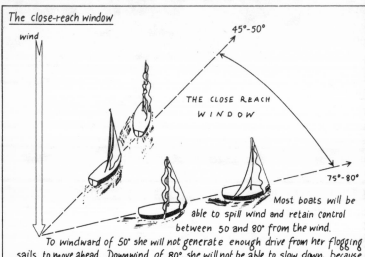

The close-reach window

wind

45°-50°

THE CLOSE REACH WINDOW

75°-80°

Most boats will be able to spill wind and retain control between 50 and 80° from the wind.

To windward of 50° she will not generate enough drive from her flogging sails to move ahead. Downwind of 80°, she will not be able to slow down, because her mainsail will be full of wind.

she stalls, her head will fall off the wind. See how effectively you can control the tendency with the mainsail, but note carefully the closest angle to the wind at which the boat will sail slowly. That is the 'high' side of the close-reaching window. So long as you can manoeuvre to put your destination somewhere between low and high, you can make an approach under perfect control.

If there are moorings in your chosen exercise area, pick one at random and try to place your boat in such a position that when you steer towards it your boat is on a perfect close reach. This is great training for wind-awareness.

Boat balance and pivoting Set the boat up so that she is stationary with the wind more or less abeam and both sails spilling. Let go the tiller. Now pull in the mainsheet and see how far and how hard she luffs.

Repeat the exercise using the jib sheet instead. Does she bear away? If so, how much, and for how long?

Now sail the boat on a reach with the true wind just abaft the beam and the sails correctly trimmed. When she is moving well, see if she will tack without touching the mainsheet. Many boats will do this adequately, but it may be a different story in half a gale and a steep sea. Do it again, only this time haul in hard on the mainsheet as the boat comes to the wind, keeping the sail drawing all the time. The difference may surprise you.

Heaving to Heave the boat to by tacking her and leaving the jib sheet fast. Don't forget to put the helm 'down' to leeward as equilibrium is being reached (a wheel will of course be wound 'up' to windward, but the correct term is still 'helm down'). Once she has settled, play with the sheets and see if you can induce her to point up or down by altering the balance of her rig.

Losing way by stalling sails See how you get on slowing the boat down by oversheeting the sails, both on a reach and down-wind. Check what this is doing to the helm balance. You may find the boat becomes hard to steer if it's a breezy day.

And so on. See what you can come up with for yourself to solve any points of interest which have arisen.

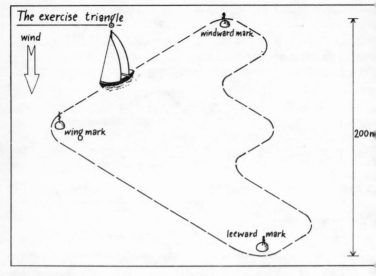

The triangle As soon as you've given yourself an insight into the boat's capacity to help herself manoeuvre, you can increase the interest by arranging a three-cornered course to sail around. One buoy should lie approximately to windward of another and a third, the wing mark, is placed out to one side so that the three form a triangle. The distance up the windward leg can be anything you like, but 200yds is ideal.

When you set up your course you'll need to be creative with what Nature or the local yacht club mooring committee have provided. With luck, you'll find a couple of buoys that will do duty as two corners of the triangle. For the third, you can always lay your kedge with a fender tied to the end of the warp.

Having set up the course, start working round it from the leeward buoy, concentrating on really *sailing* the boat. Make lots of tacks as sweetly as you can; ditch the mainsheet as you bear away round the top mark; gybe tightly and without drama at the wing; trim immaculately down the reach, then harden up both sheets as you nip back round the leeward mark to start again.

When you've got the idea, see if you can manage it without passing more than a boat's-length from the buoys. Then half a boat's-length. As soon as you've achieved that you can time yourself and start a serious competition. After an hour you and your crew will be banged

74

out, and you'll have learned more about sailing than most folks pick up in a season.

When you are confident that you can do it as fast as an America's Cup crew, see how slowly you can manage, without ever losing control or hitting a mark. That'll stop you feeling too pleased with yourself. . . .

The man overboard game This is the best exercise in the world for teaching wind-awareness, and the sense of tactics vital for successful boat handling under sail. There are many different ways of manoeuvring a boat back to a person in the water. This is only one of them. It also happens to be about the best, but *only if you're a good sailor*. We'll go more deeply into this whole subject in a later chapter. For now it is an exercise and nothing else:

* Get the yacht moving fast on any point of sailing and throw the dan-buoy (or a bucket and a fender tied together) over the side.
* Detail someone to watch it, lest you should become disorientated and lose sight of it.
* Immediately sail the boat away, properly trimmed, on a *True Beam Reach*.
* When you've enough room to manoeuvre, either tack or gybe. Bear in mind that tacking will take you further up-wind. Gybing will lose you ground. Either may be what you want.
* Steer the boat towards the dan-buoy and see whether or not she is on a *Close Reach* within the limits you have defined for her. (Don't forget to dump the centre boom-vang if necessary).
* If she *is* on a close reach, lose way and slowly approach the dan-buoy.
* If she's 'below' a reach (i.e. to leeward of the desired heading, or too hard on the wind), make all the ground you can close-hauled, 'above' the target, before bearing away and spilling wind on your final, close-reaching approach. Failure to do this will result in the boat's stalling into the windward sector as soon as you try to slow down.
* If she's 'above' the desired heading (you'll know this because you won't be able to persuade the mainsail to spill wind properly), you must bear away sharply, run down-wind for a few yards, then steer

75

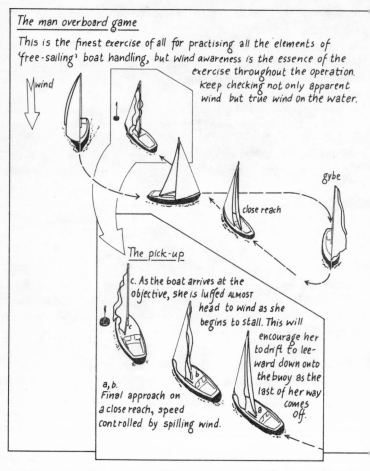

The man overboard game

This is the finest exercise of all for practising all the elements of 'free-sailing' boat handling, but wind awareness is the essence of the exercise throughout the operation. Keep checking not only apparent wind but true wind on the water.

wind

gybe

close reach

The pick-up

c. As the boat arrives at the objective, she is luffed ALMOST head to wind as she begins to stall. This will encourage her to drift to leeward down onto the buoy as the last of her way comes off.

a, b.
Final approach on a close reach, speed controlled by spilling wind.

once more for the buoy taking another look at your angle to th
wind.

* The reason why you sailed so far away from the dan-buoy on th
initial beam reach was in order to have enough sea-room t
execute either of these last two manoeuvres if they should b
required. Do not waste that ground through indecision.

To reiterate: as soon as you have tacked or gybed, steer for the buo
and let all sheets right off. You will be in one of three situations: i
you are well above the close-hauled line but all your sails will spil

wind, you have it made. If the mainsail *won't* spill, you must bear away smartly before heading back up for the buoy again and reassessing your chances. If you are too near to being close-hauled, power up-wind for a few yards before bearing away on to your final approach. Whatever you do, there is no time to lose.

* As for picking up the buoy, you'll discover that if you stop to windward of it with the breeze well out on your weather bow, the stalling boat will slide down towards it, particularly if you put the helm right to leeward to luff off the last of her way. You'll then be able to pick it up amidships. Watch out for the flogging jibsheet, though. If you've a roller genoa, furl it before you go out on the deck.

Finding that close reach in the heat of the moment requires judgement of a moderately high order. Don't be disheartened if this exercise seems hard going. Try it again after a few months, but stick to one of the other man overboard methods if there is an emergency in the meantime.

Don't ever kid yourself, however. Until you can do this, you can't really sail. An able boat handler can pull it off any time, day or night (with a floating light), in fair weather or foul, in any boat within reason.

That's something well worth aiming for, but without practice, you'll never get there.

CHAPTER TEN

Moorings

Mooring buoys are like hats: they come in all sizes and fulfil a multitude of functions. Some are small, others are large; some are inconspicuous, others stand out like an Ascot bonnet. Many are designed purely for lightweight use on summer afternoons, but some offer security in the worst of winter gales.

When you pick up a strange mooring, deciding what you've got is the first priority. Unless you can find a reliable local who knows its recent history, you'll have to trust your own judgement on such questions as whether or not it is intended for a boat of your tonnage, and if it has seen any maintenance since Eve ate the Apple.

When you are approaching a mooring buoy you should assess in plenty of time what will be the means of securing your bows to it. Does it have a pick-up buoy to beckon your boat-hook? If so, then in all probability it will also supply a chain, or strop of some description to make fast to your foredeck cleat, or samson post. If there is no pick-up buoy, you must be ready with a length of line of your own; *ready* being the watchword. You'll probably opt for rigging this line as a slip (i.e. through the ring in the buoy and back to the boat again) to begin with, because the helmsman may not make life easy for the troops on the foredeck and the last thing they'll want is to be tying knots with their cold fingers. You will need up to 20 ft of line for the initial job. No more. Don't have a large heap of rope all over the foredeck waiting to foul on something, or be dropped over the side into the propeller. If your rope is long, make the bight fast on one cleat so you've 20 ft of free end to work with. Lead this out through the fairlead, over the roller, or whatever your boat provides; you are then ready to pass it through the ring on the buoy, bring it back aboard, take up the slack, and make fast.

When the slip is on, you can organize matters to suit the occasion.

If you're stopping for lunch on a calm day, just lie to the slip. If you are staying overnight, by far the best thing is to shackle your anchor chain to the buoy, but leave the slip on for handling purposes. You can pull most buoys right up to the stemhead with the slip while you shackle on the cable. If you wire the shackle, you are as safe as the buoy is. There are just two problems: the first annoyance with 'chaining up' is that the noise may drive you to the false comfort of the medicinal bottle; the second is that if you need to leave in a hurry, a wired shackle may prove less than ideal.

The alternative way to secure to a buoy with a ring is to use a stout warp secured with a *round turn* and a *long* bowline. The round turn is to kill any chafe, and the long bowline is used so that you can reach the knot without having to adopt too obsequious a pose. The slip is left on for handling purposes.

MOORING UNDER POWER

Calm conditions   Approaching a mooring where no tide is running and there is no significant breeze is simplicity itself. Just remember that if you rush at the job and then gun the engine astern, you're going to prop-walk the bow away from the buoy. So take it easy.

As in all mooring pick-ups it pays to decide early which side of the bow you will lay on to the buoy. It is far simpler for the boat-hook operator to grab the mooring if you stop the boat with the buoy somewhere between the stemhead and the main shrouds. Tell the crew which side, and all will be peace.

Strong winds   If it is blowing hard, you'll have to approach the buoy from down-wind. Bear in mind, however, that as the boat slows down she is likely to stall. If she is head to wind, you may experience problems keeping her head up at the end of the operation, which will result in an unseemly scrabble over the pulpit to grab the buoy as it disappears to windward. It is preferable in these sorts of conditions to finish your approach with the wind 10° or so on one bow, and choose the lee bow to lay against the buoy (assuming the buoy is of a soft material). Then, as you slow down, the boat will be certain to stall into the buoy rather than be running the risk of falling away from it.

If the buoy is made of steel you won't want to bash your topsides on it, so the only answer is a straight up-wind approach. Be aware of the fact that the boat will blow away sideways soon after she's stopped. If you've overrun the buoy at all, make sure that you stall away from it after the rope is on.

Strong tides   Given that you have arranged for an up-tide approach, this is by far the easiest condition in which to moor. There are no problems of blowing around once you've lost way because, relative to the water, you are still moving. So, of course, is the mooring buoy. All you have to do is to 'nail' the buoy on to an object behind it when you are still some distance away on your final approach. It doesn't matter if you are coming partly across the tide. Once this transit is established the boat has only to be kept on it for success to be assured. As with all pick-ups, decide which side of the bow you'll put the buoy on, then, when you are right up with it, come head to tide with the buoy placed as advertised.

Keep the boat moving through the water until the crew have completed their task. The job isn't finished until they have called out the 'All fast'. If you allow the boat to sheer across the stream while they are still working, they may be unable to hang on. Maintain your station carefully by using new transits: one pair ahead of you and one pair abeam. Keep both of these 'on', and you are solidly placed as the mooring itself. The crew will have an easy time making fast, and they'll never know why.

Wind across tide   This is always the interesting one, and there is no 'off-the-peg' answer. Generally, however, tide will prevail over wind in the case of a deep-drafted sailing vessel. Look at the way any other moored boats are lying. If you approach at a similar angle to craft like your own, you won't go far wrong. Just remember to pick a transit behind the buoy and *keep it 'on'*.

Slipping under power   When you are leaving a mooring under power it is important to be sure not to foul your propeller on either the mooring itself or, more likely, the pick-up strop. The simplest way to be certain is to let the boat blow away from the buoy before engaging the gears. If there isn't the wind for this, you can always go astern.

Sometimes, the proximity of neighbouring vessels, or the state of wind and tide, dictate that you must leave by going ahead past the buoy. If so, you have a choice: you can give her enough of a sheer to clear the mooring, and then swing the stern away from it as you go by, always remembering that it is your propeller the rope is looking for, and that the boat pivots around her keel. The other method is for the crew to walk aft along the side-deck still hanging on to the mooring as you motor away. When he is standing on the quarter, he releases it, ensuring that it falls well clear.

MOORING UNDER SAIL

No tide   Mooring under sail in slack water is by far the most difficult of the various possibilities, just as it is under power. The reason is the same, too. The boat must be brought to a virtual standstill at exactly the right spot.

The surest way of doing this is to approach the mooring on a close reach, going as slowly as you possibly can (Chapters 6 and 9). The aim should be to stall the boat just as the buoy is nudging the lee bow, but a neater result will be obtained if, instead of sailing directly towards the buoy itself, you close-reach towards a point a few yards to leeward of it, then just before you are dead down-wind of the buoy, luff up to it, taking off the last of your way as you do so. Make sure that the buoy is on the designated side of the bow though, or the boat-hook platoon won't thank you.

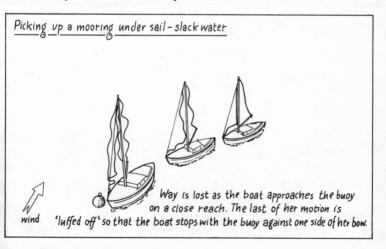

Picking up a mooring under sail – slack water

wind   Way is lost as the boat approaches the buoy on a close reach. The last of her motion is 'luffed off' so that the boat stops with the buoy against one side of her bow.

On most boats you'll be better off doing this under jib and main, but if you are fortunate enough to have a yacht that will close-reach under main alone, it may pay you to take the jib down in good time. The foredeck crowd will have less unpleasantness if you do. They don't like having their ears boxed by the clew, although the close-reach approach does keep this to a minimum.

The roller jib scores high points here. Have just enough jib drawing to maintain drive, then when you are confident that you don't need the sail any more, roll it away.

Wind with tide   The only difference between this and the no-tide situation is that you'll have to pick a transit in good time to be sure you don't get set below the buoy. You may find it more difficult to pick a close reach, however. The dynamics of the situation will speak for themselves, but remember that because you are being swept down-wind by the tide, you will do well to start from 'higher up' than you would otherwise have done. Don't be too concerned about overdoing this; it's easy enough to lose ground when you are nearer the buoy by luffing into the tide, or spilling wind to slow down. If you judge things correctly, you will slide across the tide on to the mooring, which will be picked up on your lee bow.

Don't forget that as soon as the buoy is hooked, you must steer straight into the tide so that the hands can bring it aboard without having to fight the boat as she sheers across the stream. Once your

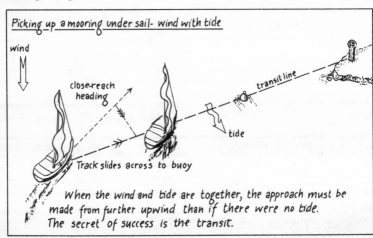

Picking up a mooring under sail- wind with tide

wind

close-reach heading

transit line

tide

Track slides across to buoy

When the wind and tide are together, the approach must be made from further upwind than if there were no tide. The secret of success is the transit.

way is off, you can't get it back as you could under power, so you must make use of what you have left after luffing to give the crew the easiest time you can.

Wind across tide   If the wind is forward of the beam, but broader than close-hauled when you are stemming the tide towards the buoy, this is the easiest state of all. You are, of course, on a good old close reach, so you can go as fast or as slowly as you like. Since you will never have to go any slower than the speed of the tide, you probably won't have to come anywhere near stalling speed. You can just nudge up towards the mooring and keep sailing on the spot while the crowd up forward make you fast.

On the other hand, if you find that when you are stemming the tide, the breeze is abaft the beam, you have an entirely different situation. You are into a 'wind against tide mooring'.

Wind against tide   It is of paramount importance that anyone who is intending to sail on to a mooring, up to an anchorage, or alongside a dock, has a working definition of 'wind against tide'. Without one, all sorts of marginal situations such as the one described in the previous paragraph will be misjudged. Chaos will be the result.

The definition is simple: assess the direction your boat will be headed when she is at rest on the mooring. If there are other moored

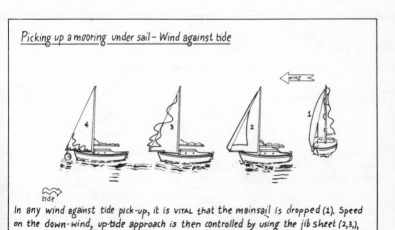

Picking up a mooring under sail – Wind against tide

In any wind against tide pick-up, it is VITAL that the mainsail is dropped (1). Speed on the down-wind, up-tide approach is then controlled by using the jib sheet (2,3,), or by dropping the sail altogether (4).

boats handy, so much the better. Look at them for the answer. Then ask yourself the crucial question: 'When my yacht is in that attitude, will my mainsail be capable of spilling wind, or will it be pressed against the shrouds?' If the answer is, 'Yes, it will spill wind,' you do not have a wind-against-tide situation. If the answer is 'No, it won't', or even 'Hmmm . . .', then you have.

The only way of stopping a boat relative to a mooring buoy is to approach up-tide, just as you would under power. If this means your main can't be allowed to flog out its wind, there is but one solution: drop it, and pick up the mooring down-wind under jib only, checking your way with the sheet (see Chapter 6). It's a piece of cake, and if you try to do the job by any other method (luffing up across the tide, for example), misery, humiliation, and broken heads from the resulting gybes on the buoy will be your just reward.

The wind-against-tide pick-up is notably sweet for the foredeck gang because the headsail is blowing away from them (or being rolled up as required) and the driver can hold the boat beside the buoy at exactly the speed of the tide while they fumble away to their hearts' content.

The lethal pick-up buoy can cause a great deal of trouble if you allow the boat to sail between it and the main mooring. This must be avoided at all costs, especially if she is in a fin-keeler. The pick-up strop will take full advantage of any opportunity you give it to insinuate itself between keel and rudder.

Slipping under sail presents no problems if you adhere to the above principles for deciding whether or not to set the mainsail on the buoy. If you reckon it is wind-against-tide, you'll have to sail away under headsail. When you've got room you can bring the boat on to a close reach and hoist the main. There is no need to luff head-to-wind for this. It only makes life difficult. So long as the sail can spill wind it can always readily be hoisted. The same applies to dropping it.

If you are surrounded by other boats and you are hoisting main and jib, you must consider from first principles what may go wrong. Remember that after you have dropped the mooring, the boat will slide sideways some distance before she overcomes her stall and begins to drive forward. If you intend to leave close-hauled this will

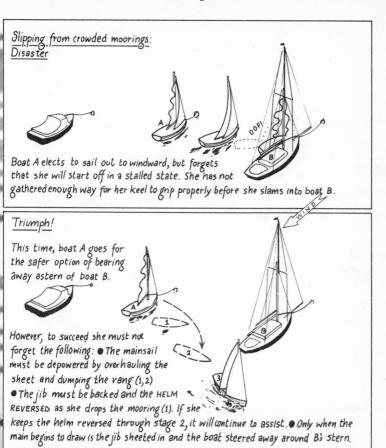

Slipping from crowded moorings:
Disaster

Boat A elects to sail out to windward, but forgets
that she will start off in a stalled state. She has not
gathered enough way for her keel to grip properly before she slams into boat B.

Triumph!

This time, boat A goes for
the safer option of bearing
away astern of boat B.

However, to succeed she must not
forget the following: ● The mainsail
must be depowered by overhauling the
sheet and dumping the vang (1,2)
● The jib must be backed and the HELM
REVERSED as she drops the mooring (1). If she
keeps the helm reversed through stage 2, it will continue to assist. ● Only when the
main begins to draw is the jib sheeted in and the boat steered away around B's stern.

be important, because, left to her own devices she may slide all the
way into the next boat. Should you decide that because of this you
won't be able to pass clear ahead of your neighbour, you'll have to
bear away hard immediately you've slipped. Without good handling,
the boat may not want to co-operate. The rudder won't be working
straight away so if you are to avoid a collision you'll need to steer
with the sails (Chapters 3 and 5). Overhaul the mainsheet to the knot,
dump the boom-vang, back the jib, and she will bear away so fast
she'll surprise even herself.

CHAPTER ELEVEN

Anchoring

THE THEORY OF ANCHORING

The art of anchoring used to be well understood by everyone who went down to the sea in cruising yachts. In recent years, however, marinas and visitors' moorings have proliferated so that for many, though by no means all of us, anchoring has become an unusual activity. The result is that a knowledge of the rudiments of anchoring has dropped down the list of priorities.

Consider the case of the yacht *Dumbo* as she comes swanning into Snugbury Bight one quiet Sunday lunch-time. She finds herself a hole amongst the fleet of moored and anchored lotus-eaters, and brings herself to a standstill. Macho Mike lumbers up to the foredeck and throws open the bow locker with a crash. He drags out an apology for an anchor, peers myopically at it to see which way up it goes, then heaves it over the bows. By a miracle of chance he has contrived to lead it through the pulpit and over the roller, so that an indeterminate length of chain is able to follow it noisily into the limpid depths of the bay. Mike snubs the cable when he thinks the anchor has touched the bottom, then, without a glance at the outside world he climbs back aft and goes below. A cork pops, and sounds of revelry filter up through the hatch.

After an hour or so, a somewhat belated sea breeze kicks in. The yachts in the bight swing gently so that their sterns are towards the beach. Not so the *Dumbo*. Her head falls off impotently, and away she goes, sideways, to pile up on the wall under the patio bar of the Snugglers Arms where the lunch-time drinkers get good value for the price of their beer.

You've probably made a mental list by now of all the things Macho Mike did wrong. Poor *Dumbo*! She never stood a chance because her

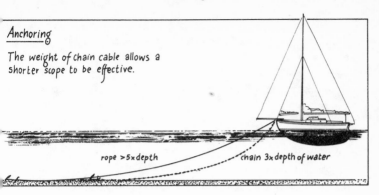

Anchoring

The weight of chain cable allows a shorter scope to be effective.

rope >5×depth   chain 3×depth of water

skipper paid no attention to any of the basic facts of how an anchor works. These are as follows:

* An anchor works by digging into the sea-bed and taking a firm hold.
* It will only do this if it is laid on the bottom and then pulled positively but carefully along.
* In order to enable an anchor to work itself into a holding position a pull with a large horizontal component is required. This means that if you are anchoring with chain, a *scope* of three times the depth of water must be allowed to run out. Should you elect to use a nylon rode with a short length of chain on the anchor end of it, you will need five times the depth of water to achieve the same result. The reason for the difference in scope is that a length of chain in the water holds itself down into a *catenary* by means of its own weight. The chain between the nylon rope and the anchor, which should be at least 10ft in length, serves to assist the horizontal component of the pull; it also provides a vital anti-chafe device against abrasion by the sea-bed.
* The scope that is required to enable an anchor to bury itself also ensures that it stays put when the load comes on. It is therefore doubly important when laying chain that the boat is, if possible, induced to move steadily away from the anchor, so that when her weight is brought up by the ground tackle, it will dig in the anchor. If a pile of chain is dropped on the bottom, the boat may lie satisfactorily to it until the system is tested, as was the case with the *Dumbo*.

87

* Somehow or other, the yacht must actively work her anchor into the bottom. If you're intending to go off watch, it really isn't good enough to leave the ironmongery lying around down there and hope for the best. You must *know* that you are properly anchored.
* Both during the anchoring process and afterwards, the crew should use transits to make sure that the yacht is not going anywhere.

CHOOSING A PLACE TO ANCHOR

Since this is a book about sailing and boat handling, rather than navigation and general seamanship, there is no need to dwell at any length on this question. Common sense should dictate whether a bay, river or roadstead will be sheltered, and be likely to remain so for the length of your intended stay. In general terms, one is looking for protection from the sea rather than the wind, since it is waves and pitching which usually pull an anchor out of the bottom. If you have chosen a site with good holding ground (firm mud, or clay is best, though sand can work well also) and have laid your anchor well, the wind should not present any problems, unless it blows up in truly horrendous proportions.

If a hard blow is expected, it is well worth selecting an anchorage which offers the potential for laying an enormous scope of cable. We are not going to consider all the possible ways of laying out extra anchors. That is a subject about which books can be and have been written. Suffice it to say that a single large, well-designed anchor dug hard in on 10:1 scope of chain cable is as near to being an ideal safety-net as you are ever likely to get.

Depth consideration   You must find somewhere to anchor in which there is plenty of water to float the boat *all round her swinging circle*, at all states of the tide. Within those criteria, the shallower the water the better, because this will allow you to use more scope if you need it, or less cable out of the locker (and less work for you) if you don't.

Swinging room   When you enter an anchorage with even one other boat in it, you can bet your favourite bower to a rusty grappling iron that she'll have hogged the best place. Well, tough luck, old son. It's first come, first served. That's the ancient custom of the sea. So you'll just have to accommodate yourself somehow. When an anchorage is

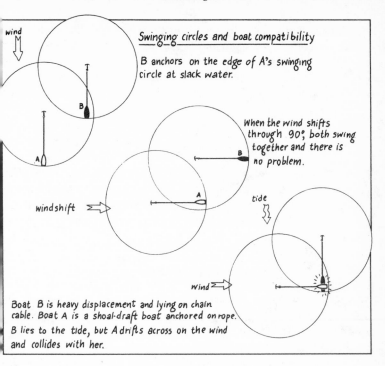

Swinging circles and boat compatibility

B anchors on the edge of A's swinging circle at slack water.

When the wind shifts through 90°, both swing together and there is no problem.

windshift

tide

wind

Boat B is heavy displacement and lying on chain cable. Boat A is a shoal-draft boat anchored on rope. B lies to the tide, but A drifts across on the wind and collides with her.

crowded you might have to anchor inside someone else's swinging circle. If you do, try to pick a boat with similar characteristics to your own, so that you'll swing together and stay out of each other's way.

Whatever the next-door boat, if she is using rope and you are favouring chain, forget it! The two are as incompatible as a snail and a bumblebee.

ANCHORING UNDER POWER

One of the improvements in life brought about by the universal auxiliary engine is that one can now be sure the anchor is holding before the matter becomes critical. As we shall see, a certain amount can be done in this department under sail alone, but if the wind is light, there may be a question-mark remaining which will only be resolved by soaked pyjama-clad sufferers, dragged from their bunks by a sudden midnight squall.

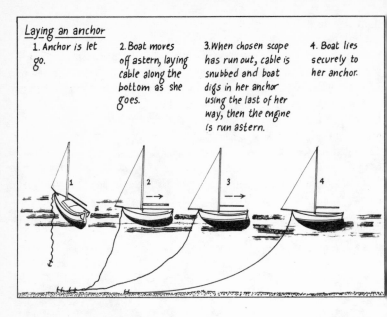

Laying an anchor
1. Anchor is let go.
2. Boat moves off astern, laying cable along the bottom as she goes.
3. When chosen scope has run out, cable is snubbed and boat digs in her anchor using the last of her way, then the engine is run astern.
4. Boat lies securely to her anchor.

Anchoring with chain The process of anchoring under power is delightful in its simplicity. The yacht is headed up to the wind, or the tide if there is any. The anchor is let go just as you begin to make sternway over the ground. Where there's a tide, it may take the boat away for you. If the water is slack it will be necessary to go astern under power.

While the boat is moving away from her anchor, cable is *laid* (not dumped) steadily so that it lies in a straight line between boat and anchor. When enough cable has run out it is snubbed and the engine is put out of gear so that the momentum of the boat begins to dig in the anchor. Now comes the clever bit. The hand on the foredeck watches the cable carefully. As soon as it looks as though the boat is about to be pulled ahead by the weight of the chain being held off the bottom, he signals the skipper to go astern. The engine is now put half astern and the boat will pull steadily on the cable. This serves two purposes: it gives the anchor the horizontal pull that it needs to work itself into the sea-bed, and it gives the crew confidence that, if it will hold with that amount of power on it, the anchor is unlikely to be plucked out by anything the coming night has to offer.

While the engine is going astern the foredeck boss should watch the cable to see if it 'ducks'. This will indicate some movement on the sea-bed. You would expect the cable to bounce a little initially, while any final kinks are pulled out, but once the situation has stabilized it should not move at all; some people like to put a hand on it and feel what it's doing. Meanwhile the skipper should be watching transits abeam to make sure the boat is not creeping astern. If she is, he can try a little more scope. If that doesn't work, he will have to pull up the hook and have another go. It may well break the surface all fouled up with kelp, or with one of its flukes stuck jauntily into an old beer can, bucket or chamber-pot.

The business of digging in the anchor should be done with the stealth of a cat-burglar. If you go blasting off astern at 4 knots, snub your cable, then expect the anchor to stop you, you deserve to be unlucky. If it holds, your problems are surely at an end, but it is far more likely to plough a shallow furrow along the bottom and never get a grip. The anchor must be worked into the mud by a combination of sensitivity and strength. Having got the knack, you'll cruise round the world and back without ever dragging.

Anchoring with warp   The only difference between the processes of anchoring with chain and warp is that when you are using rope it becomes even more vital that you dig the anchor in. This is because, unlike chain, rope has no damping properties. Each time the boat surges about on a gusty night she tugs at her anchor, while the yacht on chain cable may well do no more than lug a bight across the sea-bed. When you are confident that the anchor has a good hold, pour on plenty of power and make sure. Then you'll sleep soundly. You can even take a drink if you fancy it. Just keep an eye on two or three sets of transits to make sure that you are staying where you should be.

WEIGHTING THE CABLE AND LAYING OUT A SECOND ANCHOR

Occasionally, conditions in an anchorage become so hectic that even with the maximum possible scope laid out for the bower anchor, you require still more holding power. The first action is to lower a weight down the cable in order to depress the catenary. The weight must be of at least 6olb to do any good, and care should be taken to guard against chafe if you are anchored on rope.

It used to be possible to purchase weights ready-made for this purpose, and beautiful items they were. In these enlightened times, however, we must make them up for ourselves.

The benefit of deploying a weight is really twofold: not only does it serve to hold down the cable and ensure that the anchor pulls in a horizontal direction, it also works wonders in damping down the boat's surging tendencies.

If you still aren't happy with the situation, or if you haven't been able to organize a weight, you must lay out a second anchor. This should be as large as is reasonably possible and should be shackled to a long nylon warp with a short (3m) length of chain next to the anchor to guard against chafe on the sea-bed. The anchor (known as a *kedge*) should be laid on the greatest achievable scope, and in such a direction from the yacht that when she is lying head-to-wind the two cables will make an angle of between 30° and 45° at her bow.

If you have a good dinghy, the best way to lay out the kedge is to hook it over the stern and row away with it, while a foredeck hand pays out the warp from the yacht. When you've manoeuvred the dinghy into the desired position, heave the hook over the side. There'll be no sympathy for anyone foolish enough to let go the anchor without checking at least three times that it is clear to drop, and that no one in the tender has a bight of cable around any anatomical appendage (feet are most vulnerable; the others are even less palatable to contemplate, though the victim never complains personally).

When conditions are judged to be too tough for boat-work, it is usually possible to motor the yacht up to the chosen spot for letting go the second anchor, gathering slack on the bower cable on the way if necessary, but in any case making certain that the propeller is not fouled. The job can even be done under sail in some circumstances.

Once the two anchors are set, the load should be evened out between them so that as the nylon kedge warp stretches, it is relieved by the increasing mass of the weighted bower cable rising up from the bottom, and vice versa. The boat will ride much more quietly, and the increase in security is a mighty leap. Yachts have survived the most savage onslaughts imaginable by making arrangements of this sort.

ANCHORING UNDER SAIL

The same wind and tide considerations apply to anchoring as to mooring. When you have chosen your spot and are planning your approach you should ask the usual question: will my mainsail spill wind if required while I am going through the whole of this manoeuvre? If the answer is 'no', or if you are in doubt, drop the sail, and anchor under jib only.

Head to wind anchoring   When there is no current, or if the wind and tide are running together, you will probably opt to keep your mainsail up until the anchor is set. The only problem you may experience if you do is that as soon as way is off the boat, her head will try to blow off the wind. If your yacht has a shallow forefoot she may swing round so far that the main will no longer spill wind, causing the boat to sail around embarrassingly. If she habitually does this, it may pay you to drop all your sails as you anchor, and allow the momentum of the boat blowing to leeward to dig in the pick when the end of the scope is reached. In the unlikely event of the anchor failing to take, you will be left somewhat legless, but in the sort of light boat where this tactic may be required, it will cause but little inconvenience to drag some sail back up again for another try.

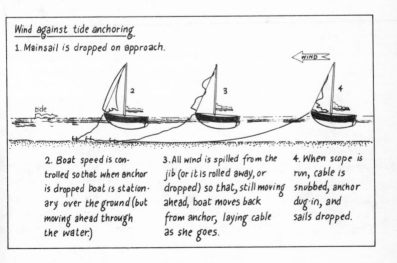

Wind against tide anchoring.
1. Mainsail is dropped on approach.

2. Boat speed is controlled so that when anchor is dropped boat is stationary over the ground (but moving ahead through the water.)

3. All wind is spilled from the jib (or it is rolled away, or dropped) so that, still moving ahead, boat moves back from anchor, laying cable as she goes.

4. When scope is run, cable is snubbed, anchor dug in, and sails dropped.

Wind against tide Once the mainsail is stowed these circumstances should cause no difficulty, so long as there is plenty of tide. With the yacht stemming the stream, the jibsheet (or better still, the furling line, if you have one) is used as a throttle to allow speed through the water to be less than that of the tide over the ground. The cable can be laid out in a straight line, and the momentum of the boat going down-tide will be enough to set the anchor. Furthermore, you'll have no doubts that the anchor is holding as the water begins to flow past the boat like a river. If the wind is strong and the tide is not, it is difficult to be sure that your anchor has taken, so a careful watch will be needed until the turn of the tide.

Digging in the anchor When under sail alone, the ideal way to dig in your anchor is to let the tide do the job for you. If there's no current running you have a choice: either you let the boat blow off until you've run out your scope, then snub the cable and hope for the best, or you sail the anchor in. If you go for the former tactic all will usually be well in strong winds where the windage of the yacht will supply the necessary momentum. In lighter going you'll need to opt for the latter if you want to be certain. There are two main ways it can be done.

(i) *Making a sternboard*: here, the anchor is dropped head to wind with the mainsail set. The main boom (or better still, the mizzen, if available) is 'backed' by physically pushing it out till it is running athwartships, and the yacht is sailing astern. With practice, and a little help from the people on the foredeck who can keep her head up by judicious control of the running cable, the boat can then be steered at a good enough speed really to feel the anchor go 'in'. The transits will stop opening as the boat comes to rest, then they'll run back again as she bounces forward on her cable.

(ii) *Anchoring down-wind*: in this alternative method, the mainsail is stowed and the boat sailed slowly down-wind under her headsail only. As she passes her chosen spot the anchor is let go. Cable is run out as she sails away. When it is snubbed the boat will quickly dig in her anchor, and you'll be left in no doubt that it is holding, because the boat will spin on her heel and lie head to wind with the headsail flogging its heart out.

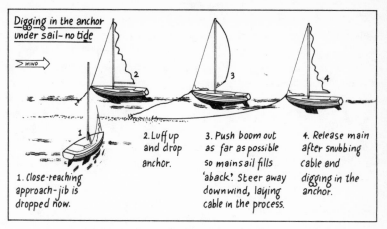

Digging in the anchor under sail - no tide

WIND

2

3

4

1

1. Close-reaching approach - jib is dropped now.

2. Luff up and drop anchor.

3. Push boom out as far as possible so mainsail fills 'aback'. Steer away downwind, laying cable in the process.

4. Release main after snubbing cable and digging in the anchor.

WEIGHING ANCHOR

Having taken such pains to dig the anchor in, you may, in due course, have to front up to the joys of pulling it out again when either the windlass, if you have one, or the foredeck crew, if you haven't, are unable to shift it. Under power this presents no problem. Just shorten up until the cable is up and down, then run the engine hard astern. If that doesn't work, give back some cable and take a gallop at it full ahead. You'll then be exerting the power of the engine, plus whatever momentum the boat has managed to build up. When the anchor is not fouled this will prove an irresistible combination. If it still won't give in, you may safely deduce that it is foul. There is then little else to do but put on the kettle and consult the manual of seamanship, or call a diver.

If you're under sail and you do not have the strength or power available to trip the anchor, you will either have to pull it out with a headsail halyard led to a tackle or to your biggest sheet-winch, or you must 'sail it out'. This is done by tacking up to the anchor, shortening cable at each board until you sail across the anchor on a short scope. As you do, the cable is snubbed and the anchor is almost bound to give up the struggle and trip out. *Great care* is needed on the foredeck while this is happening, especially if the cable is all chain.

There are no special awards for working out why this should be.

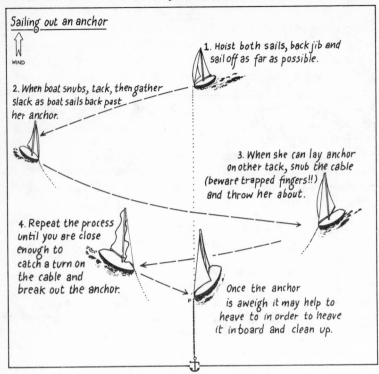

Sailing out an anchor

WIND

1. Hoist both sails, back jib and sail off as far as possible.

2. When boat snubs, tack, then gather slack as boat sails back past her anchor.

3. When she can lay anchor on other tack, snub the cable (beware trapped fingers!!) and throw her about.

4. Repeat the process until you are close enough to catch a turn on the cable and break out the anchor.

Once the anchor is aweigh it may help to heave to in order to heave it inboard and clean up.

KEDGING

When you are sailing a longish coastal passage in an area where tides run hard, it sometimes becomes advantageous to anchor during the periods of foul tide, especially when you are trying to work to windward in light airs.

A cruiser beating to windward at 3½ knots of water speed will have a Vmg (Velocity made good to windward) of about 2 knots. In a fair tide of 2½ knots this represents 4½ miles made good in an hour. Once the tide turns foul, however, progress is reduced to zero or worse if you have no engine, or are disinclined to make use of the one you have.

If the water is reasonably calm it now makes all the sense in the world to anchor or, as it is called in these circumstances, to kedge.

Using the boat's lighter anchor for convenience it is often possible to kedge in water far too deep for the best bower and its chain cable. Tie all the available rope together, then bend this conglomeration on to the end of the official kedge warp, and the depth in which a well-equipped cruiser can kedge is astonishing. Racing yachts have been known to do it in 35 fathoms of water by using all their spinnaker sheets, guys, kedge warps, dock lines, genoa sheets, etc. The biggest problem at such depths becomes the friction of the water running past the kedge warp itself, but it is always worth a try if you are losing ground and cannot fetch an anchorage where the depths are more readily dealt with. If your kedge drags, remember, nothing is lost but a few miles made good.

MOORING STERN-TO

In certain parts of the world, mooring stern-to with the bows held off by a well-laid anchor is the normal way of berthing. This method is popular in the crowded harbours of the Mediterranean and in Scandinavia, where steep-to rocky shores encourage one to berth as close in as possible. In the Caribbean the technique is used in places

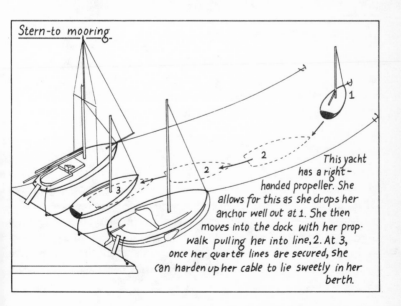

Stern-to mooring

This yacht has a right-handed propeller. She allows for this as she drops her anchor well out at 1. She then moves into the dock with her prop-walk pulling her into line, 2. At 3, once her quarter lines are secured, she can harden up her cable to lie sweetly in her berth.

such as the Pitons at St Lucia and English Harbour in Antigua.

The essence of the operation is to establish which berth you will enter, then lay your anchor in a position at right angles to the quay wall. The wall is approached by going astern until you are close enough to send two quarter lines ashore; once these are secured, the cable is shortened up so that the yacht is held at the desired distance from the quay. If you favour a gang-plank or *passerelle* it can now be rigged so that you may step ashore in splendour. The only other options are the dinghy, the tight-rope, the long-jump, or mooring too close for comfort.

There are one or two points to note about stern-to mooring. The first is that because the pull on the anchor may not always come in a straight line (in a cross-wind, for example), it must be allowed the maximum possible scope. If the harbour is crowded it is important that you use chain cable. The chaos that would result from a small port criss-crossed with taut anchor warps is easy to imagine and vile to contemplate.

If your boat is difficult to steer astern, make sure that you give careful thought to the question of her natural tendencies before laying your anchor. Failure to do this may leave you embarrassed athwart the hawse of what could have been a friendly neighbour. You may find, however, that careful use of the windlass brake and clear liaison between helm and winch-man will help to keep an otherwise headstrong yacht under tight control as she drops into her berth. Beware, though; shame awaits the mate who snubs the cable completely before he is told. Once this happens in a cross-wind all is lost, and the only remedy is to weigh anchor, fire the mate, and start all over again.

If you anticipate a strong blow from one side or the other, either lay your original anchor in that direction, or row out another anchor somewhat to windward in order to relieve the strain.

Fouled Anchors   are a common menace where stern-to mooring is the regular practice. If you discover someone else's gear over either your cable or your anchor itself, the solution is generally to make fast the end of a short line somewhere on your foredeck, lead the other end under the bight of the foreign cable, and lift it (either by main force or by winching) so that it comes clear of your own. Your anchor will heave up sweetly on nine occasions out of ten.

Where a number of large yachts have all laid out a pair of anchors in a tight harbour, trouble is guaranteed, and the results can be most gratifying to the uninvolved observer with a well-developed sense of mischief.

CHAPTER TWELVE

Operating in Tidal Rivers and Tight Harbours

It's a delight to work into a river at the end of a rough passage. The sea goes down instantly and the wind generally eases as the boat travels further inland. Crews relax, beer-cans are popped, and before you know it the poor old yacht is more vulnerable than she has been all the way across the briny deep.

Most navigable rivers are full to the banks with things to hit, and if you find one that isn't, it's probably off the chart and abounding with shoals. Fortunately for us, all that is required to avoid these unpleasantnesses is concentration, and an awareness of the sort of places where they may lie. Sailing in rivers is far more fun than hammering about in the open. There is more to see, more to do, and there are no waves to spoil it all. It's a shame to see a handy cruising yacht drop her sails and start the diesel just because she has to make a few short tacks. Today's sailing boats are more capable of delivering the goods than anything the world has yet seen. They offer the competent boat handler a unique opportunity of achieving what we are all out there for: the satisfaction which attends the completion of a job well done.

Whether sailing or under power there are a few rules that are axiomatic to river navigation, particularly when there is a current running.

Watch transits constantly Any buoy, pile, withy, drying rock, anchored vessel, vessel under way, or anything else in the water is a potential collision, whether you are headed for it or not. Regardless of where you think you are steering, the whole body of water is moving inexorably along. Here, more than anywhere, you are at risk of being set into an object you fancy you are clearing.

Noting transits is never a problem in a river, because there are

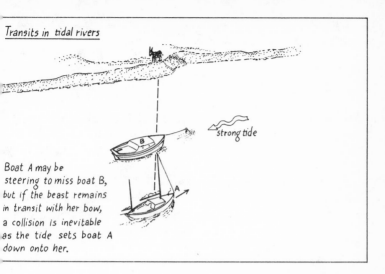

Transits in tidal rivers

strong tide

Boat A may be
steering to miss boat B,
but if the beast remains
in transit with her bow,
a collision is inevitable
as the tide sets boat A
down onto her.

always plenty of conspicuous trees, factory walls, lamp-posts, thatched cottage corners and other salient items from which to make your selection. If the 'target' is moving relative to the background, then at least you are not going to hit it with your head. Bear in mind that you are not checking transits from the bow and the stern of your ship, but from wherever your eye happens to be. Whether the whole of your boat will clear the danger will be a question of judgement.

Your own masthead is potentially at risk of fouling an obstacle. Many an unwary mariner has been brought up short as his tricolour light smashed against the top-mark of a navigation pile.

Watch out always for movement of the masts of other vessels. If you are approaching a marina, one mast creeping around among the forest may indicate that a fresh obstruction to your safe passage is about to pop out.

Do not bunch up   Boats that ruck together are a frequent nuisance late on sunny Sunday afternoons in popular yachting venues. Every boater in the area converges on the landfall buoy at 1600, bent on being away in the car by sunset. The motivation for this is clearly a desire to beat the traffic jam of yachtsmen rushing home to the dubious reality of Sunday evening TV, and the office the following morning. The result is a different sort of traffic jam in the river, but one which bears an annually increasing resemblance to the sort of nonsense we now suffer on the highways.

At the front, Joe Soap is toddling along at 4 knots, enjoying the peace. Coming up astern of him at the maximum permitted speed surge a variety of vessels under power. They all bunch into a gaggle which leaves no one any of that vital commodity, contingency space. One unexpected incident can turn the procession into a pile-up. Add to this mix that depressing ingredient of the Human Mistake who is too important to obey the rules and who comes barging through the flock at 8 knots, pulling his wave behind him. Now you have a reliable recipe for extra insurance business.

Don't involve yourself. Stay away from 'Tunnel-Vision Terence' and the bejewelled popinjay with the 'Turbo' stickers. You don't need these people. Let them squeeze one another out. Being in that much of a hurry has nothing to do with boating. If you let them, sooner or later they'll jam you into a position from which not even the snappiest seaman could extricate himself.

Look astern   as well as ahead, especially if you are taking things gently. If another vessel is wanting to overtake, give her as much room as you safely can.

RIVER SAILING

Choice of sails   Despite any urge you may have to go fast, when navigating in a river it is more important to see where you are going. You should also be carrying enough sail to control the boat, but not so much that decisions are forced upon you more quickly than you might wish. Deck-scraping genoas are definitely out. You need a high-cut jib, ideally with a long hoist for good lift characteristics, but no deep overlap. The high clew will ensure forward vision for the helmsman, and the shallowness of the sail from luff to leech will make life easy for the crew if there is any short-tacking to be done.

Tactics   If there are no constraints to the contrary (such as other vessels under way), the windward side of a river is the favoured choice, particularly if the wind is forward of the beam. Wind direction becomes unstable as you travel further inland. Having the breadth of

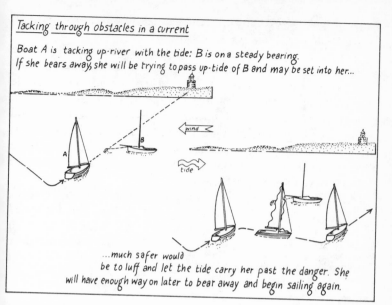

Tacking through obstacles in a current

Boat A is tacking up-river with the tide: B is on a steady bearing.
If she bears away, she will be trying to pass up-tide of B and may be set into her...

wind

tide

...much safer would
be to luff and let the tide carry her past the danger. She
will have enough way on later to bear away and begin sailing again.

the river 'in hand' to windward may make all the difference if you are unexpectedly headed.

Working to windward   Here, most of all, it is vital to keep an eye on your transits if streams are running hard. Suppose, for example, you are doubtful about whether you will clear a moored vessel on this tack. The tide is setting you up nicely, but even so you are unsure. Perhaps going about looks inconvenient. You are then left with a choice: either you bear away or you luff up. If luffing will put the tide more behind you, it is probably the right thing to do because you will then pass on the down-tide (safe) side of the obstruction. Bearing away might have been the answer if there were no tide running, but to bear away on to the up-tide (dangerous) side of the moored vessel could leave you open to being set into it.

   Always think at least two tacks ahead. Failure to do this may place you in a blind alley, whereas a modicum of foresight could have kept you clear, perhaps by going about early on a previous tack.

Lee-bowing   If you are working to windward in a foul tide and you are almost able to lay the course up a stretch of river with your sails

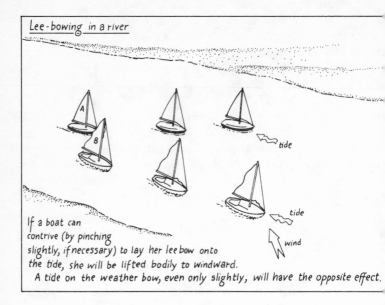

Lee-bowing in a river

If a boat can contrive (by pinching slightly, if necessary) to lay her lee bow onto the tide, she will be lifted bodily to windward.
A tide on the weather bow, even only slightly, will have the opposite effect.

well full, great dividends are available if you are prepared to 'pinch' just a little. Persuade your boat to present her lee rather than her weather bow to the tide, and she will be pressed to windward rather than being shoved down the proverbial tube. This will enable her to lay the stretch in one tack. Even if the high pointing has slowed her down a trifle, and marginally increased her leeway, her gains will more than offset these minor losses.

Tacking The importance of efficient tacking increases in direct proportion to the number of times a boat is to be put about in a given distance. At sea, 10yds lost because the boat is allowed to stall will not be a hanging matter. Ten yards in a couple of miles is not much by any standards. In a river 100yds wide, however, 10yds given away each tack may be a serious matter, so make sure that you do not sag off while the jib is being winched in. Keep way on, steer high until the jib is setting on the new tack, and you'll slice up the river in a series of powerful boards instead of a shambling, hesitant worm-track.

Huffling or the 'Gravesend Hitch', as Thames bargemen used to call it, is a specialized form of tacking, used only in rivers. It is useful in a foul tide for making ground along the edges of the navigable water where the stream is slacker. The boat must be moving well, but instead of throwing her smartly through 'stays', she is held head to wind in order to carry her way as far as possible before filling on the new tack. Care is needed not to lose so much way that a stall is inevitable as the jib fills. This is a skill that requires some practice, but it will certainly repay your trouble.

Huffling works in rivers because the water is flat and the yacht can carry her way unhindered. At sea, it is not an effective technique because the waves will rapidly knock the boat to a standstill. In any case, as we have seen, a gain of 10yds in a couple of miles, even if it were available, is hardly of measurable importance.

Grounding is most likely to occur when you are tacking in a river because the temptation to go too close to the bank is often irresistible.

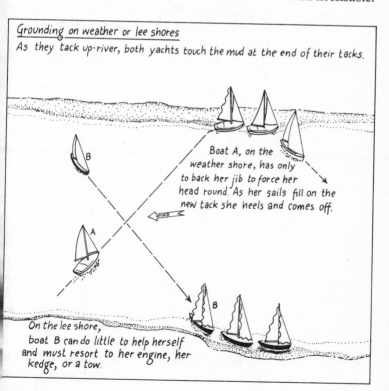

Grounding on weather or lee shores

As they tack up-river, both yachts touch the mud at the end of their tacks.

Boat A, on the weather shore, has only to back her jib to force her head round. As her sails fill on the new tack she heels and comes off.

WIND

On the lee shore, boat B can do little to help herself and must resort to her engine, her kedge, or a tow.

There are two rules about grounding on a muddy bottom:

(i)   Never go aground on a falling tide.
(ii) Never go aground on a lee shore.

The instant reaction if you feel your boat touch at the end of a tack must be to jam the helm down. It is of paramount importance to swing the boat's head through the wind before she loses way. As soon as her head is into the wind's eye, you can back the jib, which should finish off the job of pushing her round. Once she has filled on the new tack, heeling will do the rest and nine times out of ten you will sail off.

If you don't manage to get through the wind, you may elect to risk bearing off and gybing round, which involves running to leeward with your keel in touch with the mud – highly undesirable. Otherwise you must start your engine or lay out a kedge with which to pull your head round, doing all you can to heel the boat artificially at the same time. Of the three options, starting the engine is usually the popular favourite, though whether you go ahead, gritting your teeth, or astern, looking for the groove you just dug, is a question only your personal chemistry can decide.

SPECIALIST RIVER MOORINGS

Moorings in rivers are often of the fore-and-aft, or 'trot', type, taking the form of either piles or buoys. Both cause problems, but the greater source of grief is undoubtedly piles.

Picking up a pair of empty piles is actually quite easy, but people almost invariably chicken out of the job if there is another pair close by already tenanted. They go and tie up to the luckless first-comer, then, if they are well-mannered, they pump up the dinghy and run out lines to the piles.

It is simpler in the long run to approach the trot up-tide and lie briefly alongside the down-tide pile while a crewman *forward of your pivot point* attaches a rope to the pile ring (round turn and a long bow line is the preferred method). Once the line is fast, you can motor on to the up-tide pile, paying out this first rope as you go. The bow is now laid alongside the up-tide pile and the helmsman maintains station with helm and throttle while the crew hitch up to it. All that then remains is to even up the lines.

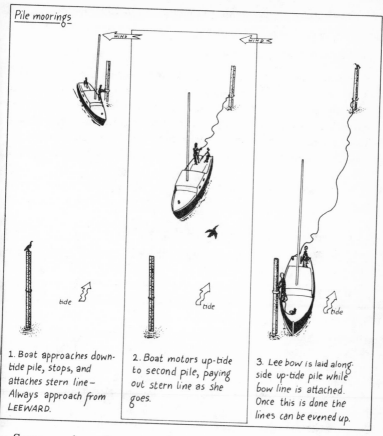

Pile moorings

1. Boat approaches down-tide pile, stops, and attaches stern line – Always approach from LEEWARD.

2. Boat motors up-tide to second pile, paying out stern line as she goes.

3. Lee bow is laid along-side up-tide pile while bow line is attached. Once this is done the lines can be evened up.

Some people prefer to rig slips rather than tie up 'permanently' to the piles. If you aren't stopping long there is much to be said for this. It is easier to leave when the time comes if your lines are both doubled back to you for instant release.

If the tide has turned, however, you might want to *wind ship* (turn around) before leaving, in which case the doubled lines will be a nuisance. Another problem a double line frequently causes is that you overestimate its length and run out of rope before you arrive at the up-tide pile. One result of this is a frenzied rush to bend yet another jibsheet to the bitter end, with Cousin Misabel fumbling her double sheet-bend in the heat of the moment and kicking the whole bunch of lu-lus into the propeller. The other is that everyone stands about

looking helpless while the yacht, securely tethered by the stern, drif
down athwart the tide in disarray.

Slips are useful, but it must never be forgotten that a slip-rope
highly prone to chafe if left overnight.

CHAPTER THIRTEEN

Warps and Fenders

It is a never-ending source of amusement to loll on a bollard near a favourite maritime watering-hole and discreetly watch the yachts securing to the wall. You can always tell the competent people. They know what they are going to do and they do it quickly, neatly and with a minimum of shouting. Then they walk away, totally confident that the boat will not misbehave. The other crews seem to leap around like monkeys in a circus act. They peer through fairleads as though sighting a competition rifle, they lead arbitrarily selected warps back as unnecessary slip-ropes; each line is made fast with a couple of half-hitches jammed up tight on the cleat or bollard, orders are bellowed concerning such apocryphal items as 'back-springs' (another circus act?) and finally, the *pièce de résistance*, the spaghetti lying around on the dock is coiled down and laid alongside the bollards – the certain pointer to the fact that this crew has not been properly brought up.

The reason for the discrepancy in performance is not hard to find. It's back to the marina again. Marina berths are such a forgiving milieu that you can get away with any old cobble-up that stops the boat hitting either end or floating off altogether. The pontoons are a convenient height for yachts, they are made of timber, they have an abundance of meaty cleats in handy places, and because they float *a yacht tied up to them is unaffected by the tide*. Most modern yachtsmen have 'learned' how to secure alongside on marina berths.

Now compare berthing against a real live harbour-wall in the west of Ireland, Northern Brittany, south-west England, or Maine. Even a quayside in the virtually tideless West Indies will probably be made of old stone blocks (if you're lucky!) studded with gel-coat-munching bolt-heads, and will very likely be exposed to a 25-knot trade-wind. What a difference. Take a liberty with your lines and fenders in

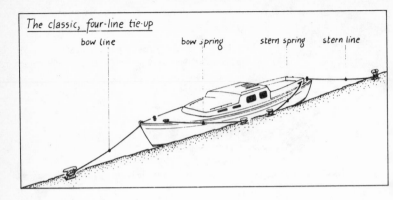

The classic, four-line tie-up

bow line   bow spring   stern spring   stern line

any of those places and you're in for expense, aggravation, or even a night spent hanging 15ft above the sea.

Even if you never intend to secure to anything other than an expensive floating pontoon, however, it is still worth doing the job right. It is quicker, neater, safer and for all those reasons it's more seamanlike.

THE CLASSIC TIE-UP

A well-secured boat has four lines on her: a headrope, a stern spring, a stern line and a bow spring. The purpose of these lines is to secure the boat in such a way that she can't move significantly forward or aft, and that she remains snugly parallel to the dock. In order to see how the four lines working together achieve this, let's take a look at what each one would do individually.

The bow line (or headrope)   secures the bow to the dock. It also stops the boat moving astern, but if she tries to do so, it will snub her bow in to the dock.

The stern spring   should run from a point well aft, and certainly from abaft the boat's pivot point. Like the bow line it will stop the boat moving aft, but if the boat is driven astern against the stern spring alone, her head will be forced off the dock and her stern pinned inwards.

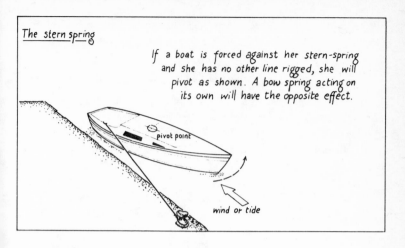

The stern spring

If a boat is forced against her stern-spring and she has no other line rigged, she will pivot as shown. A bow spring acting on its own will have the opposite effect.

pivot point

wind or tide

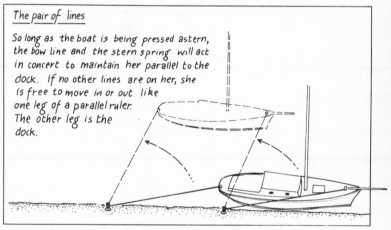

The pair of lines

So long as the boat is being pressed astern, the bow line and the stern spring will act in concert to maintain her parallel to the dock. If no other lines are on her, she is free to move in or out like one leg of a parallel ruler. The other leg is the dock.

These two lines acting together prevent any movement astern, but they also work to keep her parallel to the dock. The spring tries to send the bow out, but at the same time the bow line is trying to jam it in. The effect is perfect balance. The boat will swivel on the pair of lines like one arm of a parallel ruler, the other arm in this case being the dock.

The stern line and the bow spring form a second pair of lines which similarly check any tendency the boat may have to move ahead.

So long as all these four lines are set up at equal tensions, the boat will sit 'pretty'.

GREAT TIDAL RANGES

If the boat is secured to a floating pontoon, her lines can be set up hard so that she remains tight against her fenders. However, if there is a large rise and fall of tide, the more length that can be given to all the lines in equal proportions, the further the boat will be able to move up and down the wall without the need to tend them. In extreme cases, however, the lines will still require attention from time to time. The boat can be helped to lie close to the wall by absorbing the slack with weights (e.g. 5-gallon water containers) on two of her warps.

SPRING-LINES AS AIDS TO MANOEUVRING

The fact that a boat forced aft against her stern spring tends to throw her bow off the dock (vice versa with the bow spring) is of tremendous value when you are leaving a berth. For maximum effect the stern spring should be led aboard right aft, and the bow spring as far forward as is practicable.

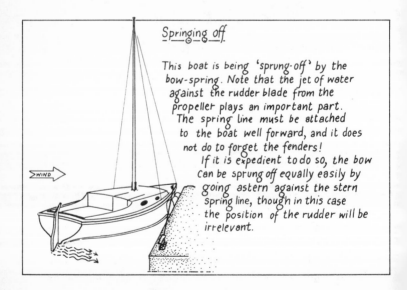

Springing off

This boat is being 'sprung-off' by the bow-spring. Note that the jet of water against the rudder blade from the propeller plays an important part. The spring line must be attached to the boat well forward, and it does not do to forget the fenders!
If it is expedient to do so, the bow can be sprung off equally easily by going astern against the stern spring line, though in this case the position of the rudder will be irrelevant.

WIND

Springing the bow off All lines are let go except for the stern spring. A fender is sited on the quarter and the engine is run astern (if there is a tidal stream setting from bow to stern the engine may not be required). When the bow is far enough off the dock, the spring is let go and the boat can be steered away from the wall.

Springing the stern off The same system is employed with the bow spring. The only difference is that the boat will spring her stern off more readily if the rudder is turned as if to steer the boat's head 'into' the dock. This is because the blast of water off the propeller will be deflected by the rudder, providing an athwartships component to its effort.

When springing off either bow or stern it usually makes matters more convenient if you double back the spring-line ready to slip it. Don't forget, if you've sprung your bow out, your stern will be hard against the dock when you start to go ahead. You will therefore need to pivot the stern off the wall for a second or two before allowing it to swing any further in as you steer away into open water. This brief 'shimmy' is rather like a football player's body-swerve, and is a sure mark of an able boat handler.

THE ROPES' ENDS

Unless you are leaving a rope doubled back for some particular reason, the immutable rules for securing a vessel to a dock are: *Short ends ashore, Bights made fast aboard. Ends coiled down on deck, One line for one job, One cleat for each line. No jamming turns on cleats.*

The reasons for these are various:

* It leaves a boat looking tidy.
* Lines can be tended from on board. It may be inconvenient, or even impossible, to reach the dock.
* Burglars will not steal the ends of your lines.
* Drunks will not trip over them and start fights.
* If you don't stick to the one line/one job rule, sooner or later you will end up with the bight running hard and fast between two cleats, totally immovable from either. What is more, you'll be driven stupid by always having to fiddle with two lines at once.

*   The sailor who stuffs two lines on one cleat will always need the
bottom one when the top one is under a heavy load.

If you are sailing short-handed there will be times when the ideal
state won't be achieved immediately, but before you consider the boat
to be properly secured, nothing else will do.

MAKING FAST ON THE DOCK

Bollards   The best and easiest way to secure to a bollard is to drop
a bowline over it.

Rings   must have a round turn to prevent chafe. Once that's on you
can use a bowline if you are certain you won't have to release the line
under load. If there's some doubt, two half-hitches are favourite. For
a bullet-proof solution, you can make a fisherman's (or anchor) bend,
then pass the tail through the lay of the standing part. But beware:
this won't let go, and may end up needing a marline-spike to undo
it.

Cleats   When the cleat is on the dock you can drop a bowline over
it, or make the line fast as you would on board.

MAKING FAST ON BOARD

Cleats   So long as the cleat is big enough, the way to make fast to
it is with a round turn, properly led so that it will not lock up, followed
by at least two whole figures of eight. There should then be no need
for a 'locking hitch'. Some cleats are too small for this, and some
modern ropes are so springy and slippery that they have been known
to work their way off the cleat. If this seems a possibility, a *single*
locking hitch may be used, *the right way round*; but *never* without at
least two figures of eight underneath it.

Winch barrels and samson posts   By far the most satisfactory
hitch to use here is the *tugboat hitch*. This is made by making a round
turn, then passing a series of bights (or loops) of the working end
under the standing part and over the bollard. At no time is a loop

passed through itself, or any other loop, so the hitch can never lock up. Like all good belays, it relies only on friction for its effectiveness.

Whenever a rope which may have to take some serious weight is made fast, consideration must be given to its lead and to whether it could possibly lock up under any foreseeable or unforeseeable circumstances. If in doubt, think again, and you will enjoy a life free of trouble and care.

At no time should the slack of a line be taken up by winding turns of the standing part over the cleat on which it has already been made fast. If the rope is subsequently loaded up this practice will result in a terminal lock-up from which the only escape is a hacksaw. Any crewman who commits this foul atrocity should have the price of a new warp stopped out of his beer-money.

THE DYNAMICS OF SECURING ALONGSIDE

Bringing a vessel alongside is one of those aspects of seamanship where communication between skipper and crew is vital. It begins with a simple, unambiguous order which tells them all they need to know.

For example: 'Starboard side to. Bow line and stern spring first, please.' (The two following chapters will explain why the skipper might have opted for those particular lines.)

The crew should now arrange their fenders at a suitable height on the starboard side (keeping one in hand, always, as a roving fender to be used when required). All four lines are led ready for action, with the two that the skipper has asked for in hand. Each line should be freshly coiled, or flaked, for smooth running.

Lines which are about to be taken ashore should have bowlines already made in them, if that's what is going to be used, and the crew should be standing with them round about *amidships* as the boat comes alongside. It is no use the bowman hanging over the pulpit. If the skipper does his job properly the boat will end up alongside, not bows-in, so that the crew will be able to step ashore easily from amidships, or by the shrouds. They should take with them as much rope as they expect to need, then maybe half as much again, *and no more*. The bight of what remains is made fast aboard so that, if necessary, they can take a turn around a cleat or bollard on the dock to defuse an unhappy situation, should one develop. If all goes smoothly, they will merely drop their loops over the dock cleats, the slack will be taken up aboard and made fast, and that will be that. The other two lines are then run out, secured, dealt with in a similar fashion, and the job is done.

If the boat is sailing short-handed, you'll have to compromise this procedure by making fast at least one bight on the dock in the initial stages of the securing procedure, but it won't take more than a few seconds to regularize the situation once the heat is off.

THE RAFT-UP

Where two or more yachts are tied up alongside each other, they should lay out springs between themselves, as well as bow and stern lines to the shore, or to the piles if applicable. It is usually helpful if they also tie their bows and sterns to one another with short *breast-ropes*. Cleats tend to be in short supply during raft-ups, so some intelligent lateral thinking may be required if seamanlike standards are to be maintained.

Boats rafted up are safer if they are organized so that their masts do not coincide. If this is not done, a sea rolling in, or a heavy wash, may result in spreader damage as the boats roll together.

UNORTHODOX TIE-UPS

Occasionally a dock offers something short of the arrangements we would like to see. An example is the finger-jetty in the illustration.

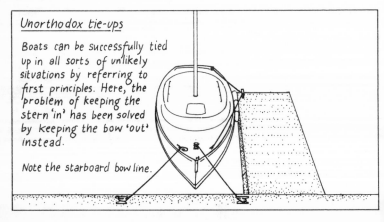

Unorthodox tie-ups

Boats can be successfully tied up in all sorts of unlikely situations by referring to first principles. Here, the problem of keeping the stern 'in' has been solved by keeping the bow 'out' instead.

Note the starboard bow line.

Unless extremes of wind and weather are anticipated this need not be a cause for gloom, so long as the principles of which ropes do what are considered. Frequently, an extra bow or stern line running off to some point on the side of the boat away from the wall is all that is required to achieve the desired balance.

CHAPTER FOURTEEN

Berthing Under Power

'Berthing under power? – easy as falling off a log!' seems to be the
general assumption. Well, it can be. Yet one sees more disasters as
yachts try to attach themselves to the dock, than in any other item on
the general syllabus of seamanship.

In the previous chapter we have neutralized the problems which
often stem from poor line-handling. So long as all hands are well
briefed on the planned sequence of events, the crew should perform
as a smooth, well-structured team. That is half the battle. The other
half lies entirely in the skipper's hands. There is no delegation when
it comes to placing the yacht sweetly alongside a berth and holding
her there while the line-men step ashore.

There are various sets of circumstances in which, from time to
time, boats have to come alongside. As we look at some of them
you'll note that the principles of success are mere applications of the
rudiments of boat handling we have already discussed. There will be
times when combinations of forces not considered here govern the
day, but this matters not a jot. Stand off and think about what is going
to happen to the boat as you go in. Work out a plan, brief your crew,
then go forward boldly.

BERTHING IN SLACK WATER

If there is no tide running, the only elemental factor to consider in
planning your campaign will be the wind. If there is no wind either
you will probably elect to dock on the side to which the propeller
pulls your stern when you give the engine the 'stopping burst'. Thus,
a boat with a right-hand propeller whose stern slides to port in astern
drive will opt for 'port side to'. That way she can approach the
pontoon or jetty at an easy 30° angle. Just as her bow seems to be

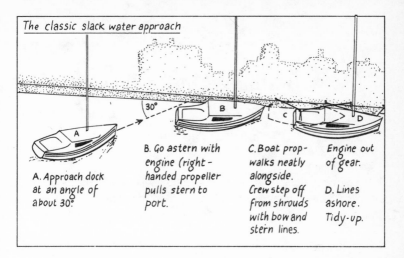

The classic slack water approach

30°   A   B   C   D

B. Go astern with engine (right-handed propeller pulls stern to port.

C. Boat prop-walks neatly alongside. Crew step off from shrouds with bow and stern lines.

Engine out of gear.

D. Lines ashore. Tidy-up.

A. Approach dock at an angle of about 30°.

overhanging the dock, turn her hard to starboard and engage astern. She should pull herself neatly in so that she stops parallel to the dock.

If, for some reason, it is impossible to dock 'with' the propeller, you should try to plan your strategy so that there is no need to run the engine astern at all. Come in very slowly at as shallow an angle as circumstances allow. If your boat displaces less than 10 tons or so the crew will be able to manhandle her to a standstill. If she is heavier they should be able to manage it by using the warps. Alternatively, you can tentatively tickle the motor astern, after first warning the crew of what may happen, and making sure that they are ready with a line to keep the stern in.

STRONG WINDS

Whenever there is a strong breeze blowing along a dock you will normally elect to arrive up-wind and let the wind take your way off, even if it means docking against the propeller.

If you are forced to come alongside down-wind this will present little problem so long as you are 'right side to'. Thus, the left-handed boat will be able to drag her way off with the engine going astern while she prop-walks her starboard side into the dock. So long as the crew are snappy with stern line and bow spring all will be well. The other pair of lines can be put on at your leisure. If you are presented

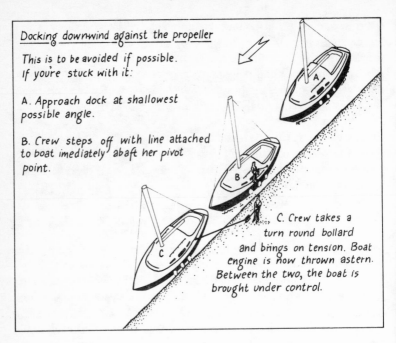

Docking downwind against the propeller

This is to be avoided if possible.
If you're stuck with it:

A. Approach dock at shallowest possible angle.

B. Crew steps off with line attached to boat imediately abaft her pivot point.

C. Crew takes a turn round bollard and brings on tension. Boat engine is now thrown astern. Between the two, the boat is brought under control.

with this situation and no dock offers itself to your favourite side, that is a more serious matter altogether. This ugly prospect leaves you a poor selection of options. Either you go somewhere else, or you must come in as slowly as you can and get your crew ashore with bow spring and stern line before doing your best to help them with the engine. These two magic ropes are now surged round the bollards to stop you and to control your boat's natural tendency to poke her bow across the tow-path.

The single docking line   Should you be faced with the above horror show with only yourself and one other crew, you'll have to use the single controlling line technique. It's not so good as the 'stern line and bow spring combo' but it will be the best you can do in the circumstances.

The line, which needs to be about one-and-a-half boat's-lengths long, is made fast to the rail (or led through a suitably placed fairlead) just abaft the pivot point. While you are coming in to the dock *as slowly as possible* your mate hops off with the rope and catches a turn round a cleat or bollard. He immediately starts surging, taking all the strain he can, short of snapping the rope. You help him with the astern-drive on your engine. With good teamwork you'll win the day, but confidence and practice are needed. Except for the unfortunates with one of those impossible down-tide marina berths, the need to do this arises only rarely, for which we should all be truly thankful.

Strong cross-winds   When there is a heavy breeze blowing *onto* the dock, the weight of wind will cause you to stall early and will blow your bow into the dock as you take way off. You'll get there all right, but it won't be tidy.

You can avoid this by docking 'with' the propeller and watching the bow carefully as you come in. Concentrate on the feel of the helm and don't be afraid to approach rather faster than you otherwise would. You need a reliable gearbox for this. If you don't have one, you should go somewhere else, or be ready for the 'bows-in shuffle'. When you are almost at your berth the boat is turned smartly to starboard if you are coming port-side to. How far she is asked to turn will depend on her discovered characteristics, but what you are after is to get her into such a position that as way comes off, her bow will

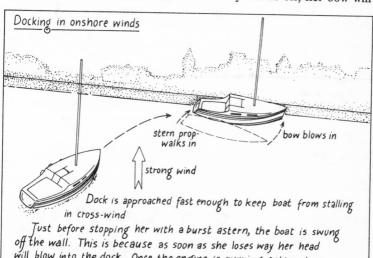

Docking in onshore winds

stern prop walks in

bow blows in

strong wind

Dock is approached fast enough to keep boat from stalling in cross-wind

Just before stopping her with a burst astern, the boat is swung off the wall. This is because as soon as she loses way her head will blow into the dock. Once the engine is running astern, her stern will 'walk' in, and her bow will blow in; the boat will then slide neatly sideways into her berth.

blow down-wind at the same rate as the stern is prop-walking to leeward. This isn't as difficult as it sounds and the boat should slot merrily into her berth. She'll be going sideways as she does, though, so plenty of fenders will be essential.

If the wind is blasting *away* from the dock your problem is entirely different. The difficulty is not so much to plant at least some part of the yacht on the wall for a second or two, but rather that of persuading her to stay there long enough for the crew to organize themselves. A heavy displacement vessel with high static lateral resistance (Chapter 1) is far easier to deal with than a lightweight flier, because she is less prone to stall and blow off at low speeds. The principle is the same for all boats, however, even if the execution varies in difficulty.

If you think there is a good chance of laying the shoulder of the boat alongside for enough time to allow your jumpers to hop ashore, you should dock with the propeller, keep as much way on as you dare for as long as you can, and be ready for the bow to blow away as you stop (*brief your crew*). The lines ashore in this case should be bow line and stern spring. Once these are set, you can motor astern against them. This will slide you back on to the wall if you've blown away from it, and keep you there while the other two lines are made fast.

If the wind is coming off the dock at an angle somewhat abaft your beam, you will be better served by a bow spring and a stern line against which, of course, you will drive slowly ahead to enjoy the miracle of the parallel ruler effect.

Use of lines and engine to pull in the boat in these sort of circumstances is infinitely more civilized than the application of 'Armstrong's Patent'. For a large yacht it may be the only way.

If none of this looks like working and your boat is light, you can always creep up to the wall bows-on, send your ship's monkey clambering ashore over the pulpit with a bow line, and worry about the details later as you try to drag the rest of the yacht bodily up to the wall.

DOCKING IN A TIDE

With a few notable exceptions, tides usually run conveniently along a dock, rather than across it. In all but the most violent winds this makes the decision about 'which side to' an easy matter. Of course, you always dock head-up to the stream.

Transits   are of paramount importance while coming into a berth in a current. If you want to arrive with your cockpit alongside the point you've chosen, line up a cleat or a crack in the wall or a stationary frog with a tree or advertising hoarding *and keep it there*. Then your approach is founded upon certainty and nothing can go wrong.

The slide   Often, you are obliged to slot your boat into a gap only just long enough for her. As often as not the space will be bounded fore and aft by expensive yachts.

Now is the time to use the tide to its full potential. Instead of approaching the wall at your usual angle, run parallel to it until you are opposite the berth, then reduce your way until you are travelling at the same speed as the tide. At this point you will, of course, be stationary relative to the dock, but moving nicely through the water, with your rudder in full operation.

You now steer slightly in towards the berth (10°–15° is plenty) and the boat will begin to 'slide' across. Watch your transits, juggle your speed so as to keep them steady, and don't forget to straighten up into the tide as you arrive alongside. Keep steering and keep your gears engaged while the crew set up the bow line and the stern spring,

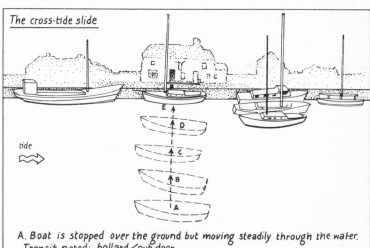

The cross-tide slide

tide

A. Boat is stopped over the ground but moving steadily through the water.
   Transit noted: bollard/pub door.
B. Boat is turned slightly so that she maintains station on her transit,
   but slides sideways (C, D) into her berth at E.

then let the yacht settle back on to these while the other lines are run out.

A refinement on the transit theme for this manoeuvre is to note two further pairs of objects: one ahead of your stationary, or cockpit transit, and one astern of it. As you approach the berth, these should open in opposite directions while your central transit remains 'on'. Then there can be no possible doubt that you are sliding into the right place.

Making a down-tide approach   This is really the ultimate recipe for catastrophe. It is only to be contemplated if there is no conceivable alternative, including abandoning the project completely.

You know the dangers. To spell them out would be superfluous.

Make sure you're coming in on your favoured side. Go as slowly as you can through the water which, remember, will add to your ground speed as it pours past the dock. Be ready with your stern line and bow spring (or single midships 'stopper') and don't forget to turn your helm so as to point the rudder towards the dock as soon as you are stationary *relative to the water*.

CHAPTER FIFTEEN

Berthing Under Sail

Berthing alongside under sail is undoubtedly the apex of the seaman's art. Performing the task well involves everything so far covered by this book, with the exception of one or two of the subtleties of power-handling. The possible variations in wind and tide are endless and it could be said that only the complete boat handler who is confidently at home with his command can promise a tidy result on all occasions. However, that should not put you off coming alongside without using your engine when the circumstances are encouraging. A strong tide with the wind against it, for example, generally makes life easy if there is plenty of space on the dock.

When the chance offers, why not have a go? You'll be glad you did when one day you are forced to do it for real.

ORGANIZATION

A well-thought-out plan is the essence of arriving under sail. Consider any difficulties which may arise during the manoeuvre, such as critical wind shifts, movement of other boats, or sudden gusts of breeze. Then give thought to everything that can go wrong on deck, because otherwise something probably will. Is the mainsheet clear to run? Have you taken up the slack on the topping-lift? Will the jib halyard foul up as it did two days ago? Most important of all, do your crew understand what's happening, why it's happening, and precisely what they are expected to do? Have they organized their warps and fenders? Is everyone clear as to who is to step ashore with the stern line, and whether he is to drop a bowline over the bollard on the dock, or surge the line to take off the last of your way?

THE ESCAPE ROUTE

We have already mentioned several times the implications of the fact that a sailing boat has no brakes. Now is when it really counts. Unless you are confident that absolutely nothing can go wrong with your scheme, you must leave a 'chicken alley' down which you can escape for another try if the sequence of events fails to live up to your expectations. There is no shame in going round again.

THE DEAD LOSER

Some berths, on some occasions, will be impossible to enter directly under sail. To a certain extent the decision about whether this is the case or not will depend upon your assessment of your own skill and judgement, but there are many set-ups that Hornblower himself would have taken one look at and sailed on by.

When you are confronted with one of these dead losers you have two alternatives: either you forget the whole thing, or you anchor off and warp in. If the berth lies to leeward of you it should be possible to ease your cable until you drop into it; if it lies to windward you will have to row a line ashore and then warp yourself up to the berth. In either case, there will be the advantage of an anchor laid out when it is time to leave. You will be able to let go all your lines and move out to the hook. Getting under way will then be a simple matter.

Liberal use of warps was one of the ways seamen of old managed to manoeuvre their unwieldy vessels into tiny harbours. They thought nothing of it because they had no choice, and if we are ever to survive without engines, that is how we must think as well. There is no way in this world that a sailing vessel of any description at all can retrieve herself from a dock that is a dead lee shore without external assistance. Lay out an anchor, however, or run a line across to a buoy, and the job presents far fewer problems to the owner of a 40-ft fin-keeled yacht than it ever did to the nineteenth-century fisherman, heaving with muscles of iron to warp his 12-ton smack off the wall.

ONSHORE WINDS

If you are docking with a wind well forward of the beam but blowing onshore you are faced with an extra factor when planning the manoeuvre. Especially if the breeze is strong or gusty, your sails are going to blow over the dock as you come in. If you are arriving on the outside of another boat they are going to blow over her as well, and both of these possibilities are undesirable. In the first place, your boom and the ironbound clew of your genoa might be spoiling somebody's paint, or braining a well-wisher on the quayside. More important, though, is the possibility that while you are still under way you will hook some static object with the bight of one of your sheets. This can be either embarrassing or expensive. It might well be both.

In general terms, this means that when the dock is a lee shore, you are better off without your mainsail, regardless of the tidal stream. The boat is trying to blow on anyway, so you are not exactly fighting to work up to weather. Most modern yachts sail adequately under genoa alone, and with careful timing you may be able to drop this just before you come up to the quay. Even if you can't, at least you've only one flailing sheet to concern yourself about.

OFFSHORE WINDS

Wind forward of the beam   When the wind is forward of the beam, particularly if the tide is running to leeward, you will have to keep your mainsail up and ready to draw until you are safely alongside with

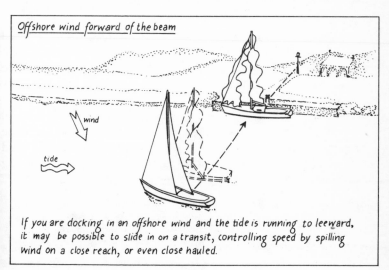

Offshore wind forward of the beam

wind

tide

If you are docking in an offshore wind and the tide is running to leeward, it may be possible to slide in on a transit, controlling speed by spilling wind on a close reach, or even close hauled.

a bow line and a stern spring on the dock. This is because if the boat is allowed to lose way so that she develops lee helm and begins to stall, you won't regain control quickly enough unless you have plenty of power available from abaft the centre of lateral resistance. Fortunately, if the wind is in this direction you'll be either beating up to the berth or on a close reach, so spilling wind to dump unwanted drive will be an easy matter.

Wind abaft the beam   The only time you will be docking with an offshore wind abaft the beam is when the tide is running to windward along the quay. The mainsail will be down but there will be no problem working the boat up to the dock. You are not trying to punch her to windward, and you will have the tide on your lee bow. This places you in the perfect position. You can slide the boat sideways into her berth just as you would under power. Instead of using the throttle to control your speed to equal that of the tide, you use the jib sheet. If you can't lose enough way because of the windage of the flogging sail, don't be afraid to drop it, then hold up a small portion of it if necessary. If it is a roller-furler, of course, the job is a complete delight.

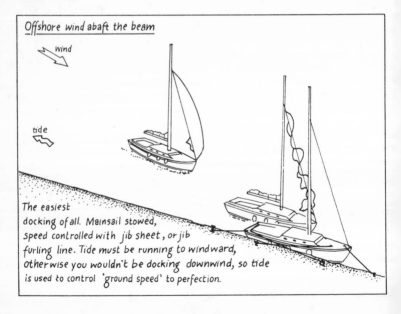

Offshore wind abaft the beam

Wind

tide

The easiest docking of all. Mainsail stowed, speed controlled with jib sheet, or jib furling line. Tide must be running to windward, otherwise you wouldn't be docking downwind, so tide is used to control 'ground speed' to perfection.

This last circumstance is one in which it is literally as simple to dock under sail as it is under power. It's probably even safer, in fact, because you can't lose your drive at a crucial moment by kicking the dog's lead over the side and into the propeller.

THE CHECKING LINE

Except in the most ideal of worlds, a yacht under sail is often carrying a little way as she comes alongside. The short line described in the previous chapter which leads from immediately abaft the pivot point of the boat is of great use here. Way can be taken off quickly and effectively by an able rope handler who steps off with this line and catches a turn around a strategically placed bollard. Once the boat has stopped moving the rope can be shifted up to a cleat or bollard on the pontoon just opposite its fairlead on the rail where it will hold her quietly while the other lines are organized.

FENDERS

It needs no imagination to see why plenty of decent fenders are required when sailing alongside. It often pays to site an extra one well forward, because if the boat is stopped by using her lines, she may find that her bow is 'snubbed in'. It shouldn't be your intention for this to happen, but in reality if often does. The roving fender is a life-saver, too, on many occasions. Always keep it handy.

One of the greatest satisfactions yacht cruising affords is to complete a passage without ever having used the engine. Such a day may be challenging, but to see it through until the boat lies quietly secured in a peaceful berth is gratifying in the extreme. There's no need to try to achieve this every time you go out, but once in a while, when conditions make it feasible, such a resounding success will add another dimension to your seafaring. Satisfaction will deepen as another link is forged with the men who wrested a living from the sea under sail alone, and who must always be our inspiration.

CHAPTER SIXTEEN

Boat Handling in Adversity

Of the four topics considered in this final chapter, 'man overboard' and 'sailing after losing the rudder' are true emergencies. Handling a yacht offshore in heavy weather, and the occasional towing job, are merely circumstances out of the ordinary where thought is required over the correct techniques to adopt.

MAN OVERBOARD

Man-overboard recovery is a two-stage operation. The first concerns bringing the boat close to the casualty and stopping her there for long enough to be able to tackle the second part, which is assisting him back on board.

Perhaps the most vital aspect of phase one is to ensure that contact with the casualty is never lost. Someone on board should be watching him the whole time. While never forgetting this essential point, there are a number of systems you can adopt for bringing a boat to rest close by, or even alongside, a crew member in the water. Which you opt for will depend on your boat, the conditions, and your assessment of your own competence. Here are three of the most effective methods:

The reach-turn-reach has already been discussed in Chapter 9. This is arguably the best of all the systems, but it has two drawbacks: to be sure of pulling it off, boat handling of a high standard is required, and it involves taking the boat away from the casualty while working up the sea-room for the pick-up approach. At night, especially if you are not certain that the victim has caught hold of the light you threw him, or if the light has failed yet again, the risk of losing touch with him in the dark may be considered too great. For all that, it is

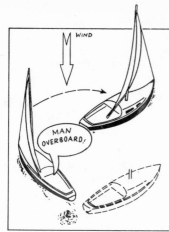

Man overboard recovery:
The heave to method

As soon as the man goes overboard,
the boat is hove to as best as she may
be on the opposite tack. The boat does
not travel far from the victim, so a
line can be thrown to him, or the
boat manoeuvred closer with sheets
and tiller.

well worth taking the time to practise this method, particularly if you
suffer from an unreliable engine, or one that will not deliver adequate
punch to manoeuvre in heavy seas. You have more sail control using
this method than any of the others.

The heave-to method has the advantage of staying hard by the
casualty at all times. As soon as the wretch goes 'over the wall' you
shove the helm down regardless of your point of sailing, bring the
boat through the wind and leave the jib aback. In theory this will
heave her to. In practice it is sometimes a messy business with bights
of mainsheet garrotting the cook as he leaps up the companionway to
join the action, but sometimes it works beautifully. Once the boat has
settled you may find you are close enough to pass a line to the victim.
If you can't manage this it is often possible to work the boat across
to him by juggling sheets and tiller.

The motor-sailing method While there is no doubt that the job
of manoeuvring to a swimmer is better tackled without resource to
the engine, the motor-sailing method will remain the hot favourite
for skippers with serious doubts about their capacity to cope with
either of the other two systems. It is also the best way to teach your
inexperienced crew to handle the boat in the event of the ultimate
horror, going overboard yourself.

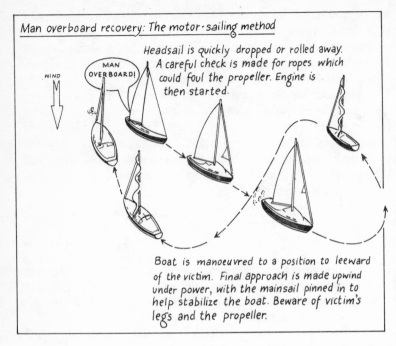

Man overboard recovery: The motor·sailing method

MAN OVERBOARD!

WIND

Headsail is quickly dropped or rolled away. A careful check is made for ropes which could foul the propeller. Engine is then started.

Boat is manoeuvred to a position to leeward of the victim. Final approach is made upwind under power, with the mainsail pinned in to help stabilize the boat. Beware of victim's legs and the propeller.

Watching the victim's position at all times, the jib is dropped to the deck or rolled away. The boat is then allowed to fall down-wind of the casualty and the engine is started *after first making absolutely sure that no rope of any description can find its way into the propeller*. The final approach is made from approximately dead down-wind with the mainsheet pinned in amidships. The sail will steady the boat and the engine should give the required control. Never forget, though, that you have a propeller thrashing around down there which can inflict shocking injuries on a swimmer.

Whichever method you adopt, always remember that if the casualty is conscious and still in reasonable condition, it is better to stop 5yds from him and toss him a line than it is to risk injuring him by coming alongside him in a seaway.

If you lose someone while you are running with a preventer on or a spinnaker set, the coolest deckwork will be needed if the victim is not to disappear from view, possibly for ever. Work out in your mind what you would do if this were to happen, then try it, and make sure your plan is feasible.

When the casualty is alongside, the next task is to hoist him aboard. In the absence of a boarding ladder you might try lowering a bight of line into the water. The tail of the jib sheet is perfect for the job. The swimmer steps in this and, as the boat rolls, he raises himself up as best he can while helpers on deck take up the slack around a cockpit winch. After two or three 'grunts' he will probably be high enough to roll under the top guardrail. The lower rail should be let go to make the job easier. It's a very fat person indeed who can't slither under the upper wire. To do so is a hundred times easier than trying to clamber over it.

If this does not work you will have to devise a lifting arrangement using a halyard, a turning block and a winch and/or a tackle (the boom-vang, detached for the occasion, perhaps?)

Patent man-overboard equipment developed in the 1980s has greatly improved the chances of both finding and recovering a crew member in the water. One such system is the 'Seattle Sling'. As soon as someone goes over the side, a buoyant lifting device which is attached to the yacht by 150 ft of floating line is thrown after him. The yacht circles the swimmer until the line is towed across him. Once in touch with the line it is easy for him to settle himself into the sling itself and be pulled alongside the yacht. This must now, of course, be hove to. Since the sling is similar to those used in helicopter rescues, the person in the water is in the best of all circumstances to be lifted aboard.

Another first-class development is the 'Jon-buoy' type of life-saving equipment. The Jon-buoy is best described as a sort of mini life raft which is launched immediately on losing a crew member over the side. The raft self-inflates and has a substantial integral drogue mechanism which keeps it stationary so that the swimmer can easily gain contact. Its comparatively large size and bright colour make the Jon-buoy easy for the watchers to spot, while its design enables the swimmer to enter it without difficulty so as to await recovery. This system can be used in conjunction with personal radio-beacons and automatic deployment arrangements which release the buoy as soon as anyone goes 'over the wall'. It proved successful in the Southern Ocean during the Whitbread Round the World Race in 1989–90.

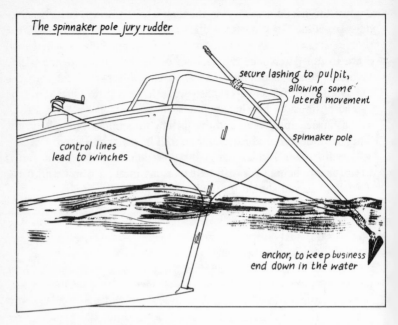

The spinnaker pole jury rudder

secure lashing to pulpit, allowing some lateral movement

spinnaker pole

control lines lead to winches

anchor, to keep business end down in the water

How successful you are on the day both at bringing the boat to the casualty and at lifting him back on board will depend entirely upon how much practice you have given yourself. Man-overboard drills should be completely automatic so that when the moment comes, you snap into action like a well-serviced machine, rather than vacillating for those vital seconds which could make the difference between life and death.

COPING WITH RUDDER LOSS

If your rudder jams hard over, you have real problems. Fortunately, it is more likely that you will lose it altogether. If you are unlucky enough to suffer this you will require a 'jury' steering system to use in conjunction with a carefully balanced sail plan. What you devise will depend on the gear you have available, but there are two arrangements which can be made using kit to be found on most modern yachts:

The spinnaker pole jury rudder The illustration is self-explanatory as far as rigging this is concerned. On a well-balanced boat, the drag of the pole alone may do the job, but if it proves inadequate, a dinghy paddle or a washboard lashed to it will help. One of the problems usually experienced is that of keeping the business end down in the water once the yacht is under way. The anchor lashed to the pole assists in this, and the added drag may improve the effectiveness of the set-up as a steering device.

The business of heaving the inboard end of the pole from side to side soon becomes tiring and that is why the control lines are fitted. They have been found extremely helpful in many cases.

When a spade rudder is lost the directional stability of the yacht will probably be so badly affected that this method won't work well, if at all. If so you should try the bucket and pole method.

The bucket and pole method   looks fanciful, but it has been used successfully. You do need a proper bucket, however. Any item of lesser quality than the pre-war galvanized clanger will fail. That is a promise. If you don't have one, you'll have to contrive another means of supplying the necessary drag.

The system works by a controlled counteraction to the boat's natural

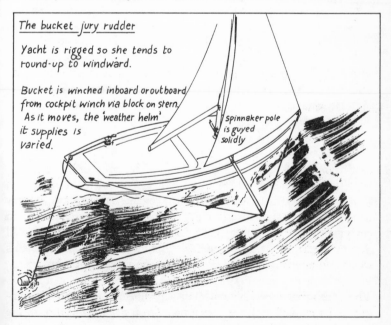

The bucket jury rudder

Yacht is rigged so she tends to round-up to windward.

Bucket is winched inboard or outboard from cockpit winch via block on stern. As it moves, the 'weather helm' it supplies is varied.

spinnaker pole is guyed solidly

tendency to round up to windward. The sails are set so that the yacht is trying hard to luff. The pole is arranged on the leeward side to encourage the drag of the bucket to counteract this. By winching the bucket inboard or outboard with the rope passing through the quarter-block, the degree of 'helm' is varied to suit the pull of the rig, and maintain a straight course.

TOWING

Approaching a disabled vessel If you are closing a vessel not under command, with the intention of passing a tow-line, you should pay attention to the fact that she will be drifting. Depending upon the nature of her disablement, she may be trailing all manner of impediments in the water, particularly to windward of her. These will catch your propeller if you give them half a chance. So don't. Assess carefully her rate of drift before you decide which way to approach her. If it is blowing hard and you come up from leeward she may come down on to you before you realize what is happening. If you approach from windward there will be the danger of fouling your propeller or of being blown down on to the casualty herself. It might well be that the safest thing to do is to position your own boat across the wind from the tow, coming up from down-wind to do so.

Having come as close as you dare to the beneficiary of your efforts, you should pass your line, or he should pass his. Which you opt for will be decided by your negotiations concerning any liability for salvage. If a disabled vessel takes the line offered by a towing vessel, she is accepting a *prima-facie* duty to pay up. The line will be hove across or, if it is too heavy, a heaving line will be used, followed by the towing hawser. This should always be long enough to allow at least a couple of boat's-lengths between the two vessels, but if the sea is rough, the longer it can be the better, because its length will damp down any snubbing tendencies. For this reason, too, nylon rope is to be preferred for its great strength and elasticity.

The towing vessel should arrange for the tow to be from the centre-line of her stern if at all possible. Tug-boats use hooks sited above their pivot points to enable them to steer properly while towing. Yachts cannot enjoy such refinements because, among other things, the backstay may get in the way. If it does, rig a towing strop with

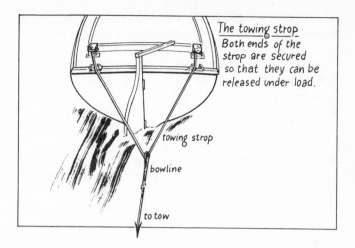

The towing strop
Both ends of the strop are secured so that they can be released under load.

towing strop

bowline

to tow

one end on each quarter and attach the tow-line to its bight with a bowline.

It is important that either vessel can release the tow-line if necessary. If you are towing on a strop, one end can be let go and the bow line will slip off, but however the tow-line is secured to either vessel, in no circumstances should a locking hitch be used, or a loop be allowed to take the strain. The line should be belayed so that no matter what the load, it can always be instantly let go.

The towed vessel should bring the tow-line aboard securely over her bow. If she has no closed fairlead it will need to be tied into whatever other arrangement is made, with a knife kept at hand to cut it loose if need be. Chafe is the desperate enemy of tow-ropes, so steps should be taken to neutralize it. A length of plastic hose is best, but if this is not convenient, plenty of heavy canvas or rags will serve for a limited period. If the loads are going to be excessive due to snubbing caused by the seaway, the tow-rope should be secured to several strong points and kept in tension. Alternatively, it could be passed around the mast a couple of times before making fast on a sound cleat. However, it should never be physically tied to the mast. If it is, you will not be able to let go once the weight comes on.

The towed boat should be steered at all times. Great care is needed when the strain is being taken up, because the pull may come in an unusual direction which will try to force the boat on to her beam ends, particularly if the towing vessel is powerful.

At all times before and during a tow, communication between the two vessels must be maintained.

HEAVY WEATHER

Sooner or later most of us are faced with riding out a gale at sea. Sometimes we are far from land and there is no choice, on other occasions shelter may be seductively close at hand, only to be discounted as being too dangerous to approach. There are various options open to a yacht caught out by stormy weather. Which tactic she chooses should depend on her sea-room, her crew strength, and on what sort of boat she is.

Heaving to in tough conditions only really works in yachts with the considerable wetted area which usually goes with heavy displacement. Such vessels also enjoy a deep forefoot which will help them to point high in the hove-to state and to make a minimum of leeway. Such a boat of 32-ft overall length can heave to comfortably in wind strengths of force 8 or 9 with an equivalent general sea state. If she is found to be making more leeway than is desirable, or if she is tending to lie beam on to the seas, she can be encouraged to fore-reach slowly by easing the headsail across, as far as the yacht's centre line if need be, though if it goes this far, it may help to bring the helm more amidships. At this point the boat will begin to sail, albeit slowly and with considerable leeway, but she will certainly be maintaining her overall windward position.

When a yacht of moderate displacement is known to be unhappy in the total, all-way-off, hove-to state, the above techniques can be used from the outset to achieve a safe condition in which to ride out a period of hard weather. The sail plan should be organized to keep its centre of effort as near the centre of the boat as possible. This can be done by using, in addition to the deep-reefed main or trisail, the staysail if the boat is a cutter, or, if she is a sloop, contriving a means of setting the storm jib on an inner forestay well abaft the stemhead. Once the rig is arranged to your satisfaction, the sheets and tiller are juggled so as to keep a minimum of way on with the boat sailing dead slow four or five points (45°–55°) off the wind and sea.

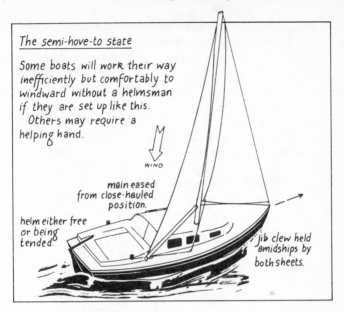

The semi-hove-to state

Some boats will work their way inefficiently but comfortably to windward without a helmsman if they are set up like this.
Others may require a helping hand.

WIND

main eased from close-hauled position.

helm either free or being tended.

jib clew held amidships by both sheets.

If you opt for this semi-hove-to technique you may well find that your boat requires the services of a helmsman. This will certainly be true if she is a lightweight yacht with a fin-and-spade profile. A yacht of this type is generally unstable when hove to because her hull form encourages the waves to knock her around. Also, as soon as she stops moving ahead, she is liable to make an unacceptable amount of leeway as a result of her lack of static lateral resistance (Chapter 1). This requirement for a helmsman is unfortunate, but to handle such a boat in this way will at least give her another option to consider at times when options may be few.

Lying a-hull When conditions become so heavy that the hove to yacht is over-pressed even by her minimum canvas, one possibility is to take everything down and lie a-hull. For a boat with poor stability characteristics this is very hazardous, but generally speaking, the sort of craft which heaves to satisfactorily in heavy seas will also be in good order to lie a-hull and will not make an outrageous amount of leeway while doing so. When a boat is lying a-hull, the helm should be lashed amidships. If you lash it 'down' and the boat gathers way, she may round up into a wave, be knocked astern and be brought up short on her rudder. Damage to the steering gear will almost certainly result.

The danger of lying a-hull is that because the boat lies beam-on to the seas for much of the time, the possibility of a knock-down must be considered. She should therefore be completely battened down, with everything properly secured both on deck and down below. It cannot be stressed too highly that for a light, flat-floored yacht in a steep, high sea, the probability of being flattened, or even rolled clean over, must never be discounted.

Both heaving to and lying a-hull have the advantage of requiring no effort from the crew. If you habitually sail short-handed and you want to be confident of taking really bad weather in your stride, there is much to be said for opting to sail a boat that can look after herself. Unfortunately, this usually means giving up some light-weather per-formance and in-harbour manoeuvrability; but then, as the philo-sopher said, 'You can't have everything in this life.'

Running off Traditionally, this has been an odds-on favourite for well-crewed boats, for the sound reasons that it reduces the force of the seas and apparent wind, and keeps the boat end-on to the waves, lessening the chance of a knock-down.

The crux of safe running is to keep your speed down. Most boats steer easily at the equivalent of their best speed to windward, so you should choose your sail area to maintain something like this speed. If it really blows you'll end up under bare poles – sooner rather than later in a lighter boat. If you're still going too fast you'll have to tow something astern to slow you down. Try long warps streamed in a bight. They work well, but they really must be *long*. 40-ft dock-lines aren't worth a cent (they aren't much good for tying up with, either).

In recent years substantial progress has been made in the commer-cial development of the *drogue*. One of these devices can be towed with dramatic effect astern of a speeding yacht. Unlike the old-fashioned sea anchor which was unwieldy, often unreliable, and always controversial, a modern drogue provides a sensible answer to a real problem which the (comparatively) flyweight modern cruiser has brought with her as one of the less desirable items in the package.

Surfing *For advanced drivers only, or the young in spirit*. If the weather is 'going your way' and you are pressed for time or feeling in need of adventure, you may find that you are able to induce your boat to surf. We have discussed the safe way to run before a gale. This is an

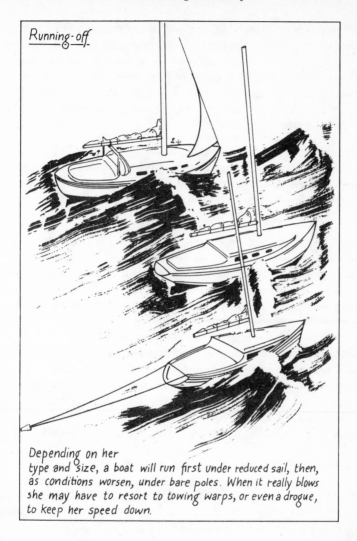

Running-off.

Depending on her
type and size, a boat will run first under reduced sail, then,
as conditions worsen, under bare poles. When it really blows
she may have to resort to towing warps, or even a drogue,
to keep her speed down.

exciting alternative, but the penalties for making a mistake are high, as a broach may well be the result. A boat which broaches at speed in a big sea can end up on her beam ends, but for all that, it must be said that life offers few exhilarations to compare with the feeling you get as 15 tons of yacht takes off down the face of a 20ft wave and goes roaring away at twice her theoretical hull speed.

The technique is easy enough, but it requires a sensitive seat to your pants: as you feel a steep one lifting the stern of the boat, luff her *carefully* about 15°. Just before the crest arrives, bear off on to a dead run. If you have caught the wave you'll be on your way, and you must now be ready for anything. The most likely event is that the boat will heel somewhat to windward which will induce her to carry on bearing away. If this tendency is not checked, a gybe-broach is the inevitable result. Firm application of lee helm at the right moment will, however, avert this horror. Once you feel the boat come upright again, hang on, and let her go. Just make sure you keep the shouts of 'Geronimo' to a minimum or you'll disturb the watch below, who are missing all the fun.

Sailing to windward Although yachts of the New Wave have proved less able than their predecessors to look after themselves, their pure sailing performance represents considerable progress. This fact can be used to their advantage in the form of one survival method that has been developed in recent years. Since the lightweight boat is unhappy presenting her beam to heavy seas, she must be kept bow or stern on. The latter is served by running off, the former by working her to windward. If she has a good suit of sails, a well-found modern cruiser-racer can be sailed up-wind under minimum canvas in very heavy going indeed. She will need skilful steering to keep her sails just on the edge of luffing, for if she is allowed to fall away beam-on at the wrong moment she may be knocked flat by wind and sea, but there are plenty of recorded instances of yachts coming unscathed through moderate gales by successfully adopting this technique.

If the boat is not powerful enough to do this, or her sails prove inadequate for the task (especially likely if she has a roller headsail), she may find she can make a working compromise by dropping her headsail, sheeting the deep-reefed main in flat, and motoring slowly ahead with the wind about 30° on the bow. The mainsail will provide some drive and will steady her. The engine will do the rest.

Unlike every other aspect of sailing and boat handling, heavy-weather seamanship is not something which is open to frequent rehearsals, but if the principles of how a yacht moves through the water have been thoroughly understood, and the necessary skills for putting them into dynamic practice have been mastered, the rising gale will hold no terrors for the skipper of a well-found craft.

Index